SIGN OF
CONTRADICTION

KAROL WOJTYLA
(Pope John Paul II)

SIGN OF CONTRADICTION

A CROSSROAD BOOK
THE SEABURY PRESS • NEW YORK

1979
The Seabury Press
815 Second Avenue
New York, N.Y. 10017

Original title: *Segno di Contraddizione*, Karol Wojtyla
Copyright © 1977 Vita e Pensiero

English translation copyright © 1979 St Paul Publications

Library of Congress Cataloging in Publication Data

John Paul II, Pope, 1920–
Sign of contradiction
"A Crossroad book."
Translation of Segno di contraddizione.
1. Retreats for clergy.   2. Clergy—Catholic Church—Religious
life.   I. Title.
BX1912.5.J6313   242'.6'9   79-4606
ISBN 0-8164-0433-X   0-8164-2048-3 (pbk)

Printed in the United States of America

CONTENTS

FOREWORD
TO THE AMERICAN EDITION

It is rare and probably unique for a Pope to have preached a spiritual retreat to one of his predecessors. Cardinal Wojtyla preached the annual Lenten Retreat in March 1976 to Pope Paul VI and his co-workers. The full text of the twenty-two conferences delivered during the retreat are presented in this volume under the original title of "Sign of Contradiction."

The words of the title are words used by Simeon (Lk 2,34) to emphasize the truth that Jesus is the great sign which needs no other confirmation, and also the sign which arouses opposition and rejection. The theme of the conferences is mankind's encounter with and acceptance of Christ, today. This theme was summarized in Pope John Paul II's inaugural address on October 22, 1978, in these words: "Brothers and sisters, do not be afraid to welcome Christ and accept his power. Open wide the doors for Christ. To his power open the boundaries of states, economic and political systems, the vast fields of culture, civilization and development."

Another summary version of the theme was given by the Pope in a later address to 10,000 young people. He urged them to look for Jesus in the Gospels; to know, to love and to live, and to be a witness to Jesus.

The retreat conferences reflect the deep faith and spirituality of the Pope, expressed with Gospel simplicity and clarity. They express sound scriptural doctrine and profound spirituality. They can serve as a blueprint for a truly active Christian life.

My best recommendation of this volume cannot possibly match the merit of its contents. Every layman, every seminarian, every priest and religious will find here an incomparable treasure of the Church's authentic teaching on knowing, loving and living Christ. This is a book of prayer, of meditation and of spiritual reading.

JOHN CARDINAL KROL
Archbishop of Philadelphia

FOREWORD
TO THE BRITISH EDITION

1978 will remain a landmark in the modern history of the Catholic Church. The death of Pope Paul VI in August was sudden but not unexpected. He had reached his 80th birthday in September 1977, and his last years were a struggle against increasing frailty. His death brought to a close more than a decade of reform and renewal within the Church which necessarily followed the immense labours of the second Vatican Council.

The election of Cardinal Albino Luciani to succeed Pope Paul was swift and dramatic. His warmth and his humility immediately endeared him not only to Italian Catholics but to the Church at large and to an astonished world. It seemed as if everyone was somehow hungry for the things of God but needed the reassurance of a smile before expressing that longing.

Pope John Paul I served the Church as Pastor and brought hope to the world for only thirty-three days. This time the grief caused by his death was heart-felt and universal. To many it seemed at that moment as if the sense of a new dawn had been an illusion.

And yet the October Conclave of 1978 gave us a Pope even more surprising than Cardinal Luciani. The world was amazed at the emergence of the first non-Italian Pope for more than four hundred years. Cardinal Karol Wojtyla was not at that time known to the general public in this country. Even Catholics here had heard his name only occasionally. In the months that have followed his election, there has been intense interest in him as a man, as a spiritual leader and as a potential force for good in the world. The publication of

Sign of Contradiction gives English-speaking readers their first opportunity to explore in depth the mind and the soul of Pope John Paul II.

The election of Cardinal Karol Wojtyla might have been surprising to the world at large, but it was not inexplicable. He had been steadily making his mark in the Church since he came from Poland as a young priest after the war to study at the Angelicum in Rome. He went to France and Belgium to visit Polish workers but took the opportunity to involve himself closely in the ferment of ideas and renewal that was then in progress. He was called back to Rome in the period before the second Vatican Council to contribute to its preparatory work. His major contribution was to the development of the theology of the lay apostolate. As the Council took shape, he played his part as a young bishop especially in determining the emphases of that important document, the Dogmatic Constitution on the Church (*Lumen Gentium*). He worked also on preparing that other vital statement, the Pastoral Constitution on the Church in the Modern World (*Gaudium et Spes*). Again he was principally concerned with developing the role of the layperson in the Church. He played a part also in saving the Declaration on Religious Liberty.

For the past decade he has been a leading figure in the international Synod of Bishops which now meets in Rome every three years. This new institution in the Church was directly inspired by the second Vatican Council. It was set up by Pope Paul VI to give visible and practical expression to the shared responsibility that bishops throughout the world have for the Universal Church. It offers advice to the Pope on major issues of the day. Cardinal Wojtyla has been associated with it since its inception. He has attended every session as a representative of the Polish bishops and has also served on the central committee of its secretariat as one of three Europeans elected by members of the Synod.

He consolidated his international reputation as a theologian when he contributed in 1974 a major paper to the

Synod on the theology of evangelisation. In Poland he had always combined a vigorous pastoral ministry with his work as a university lecturer. He had written books and contributed a great number of articles to learned periodicals. He was known for his work on ethics, on the duties and responsibilities of married life, and on the implications of the second Vatican Council.

There was another aspect of him which had also attracted attention far beyond the frontiers of Poland. People could see that not only was he a profound and scholarly thinker, but that he was a man of prayer, of faith and a sure guide in the ways of the Spirit.

For these reasons he was invited to Rome during Lent 1976 by Pope Paul VI. The Pope asked him to lead the annual Retreat made by the Pope himself and his closest collaborators, the members of the Vatican Curia. *Sign of Contradiction* was Cardinal Wojtyla's response to that invitation.

Sign of Contradiction is a sustained and prayerful reflection on the central question confronting Christians today, the question posed by Jesus Christ to his followers: "Who do men say I am?" The world is unfailingly fascinated by the person of Jesus Christ. Believers are everywhere becoming convinced that their faith must be based on Christ, centred on Christ. As Cardinal Wojtyla says: "the mystery of man is explained in the mystery of Christ. ... All the essential problems of man find tangible expression in the Christ of history."

Cardinal Wojtyla's reflections are rooted in Holy Scripture. They are nourished by a wide scholarship. They are faithful to the thought of the second Vatican Council. They reveal the strong faith of Polish Catholicism. In these pages, meditations on the Rosary and on the Stations of the Cross are completely at one with profound considerations on the truth and dignity of man.

This is not an easy book. It requires and repays careful reading. It brings a message of Christian hope but not of façile optimism. Cardinal Wojtyla concludes the retreat by declaring: "our times are marked by a great expectation"; he describes our age as "a new Advent ... a time of expectation and also of one crucial temptation – in a way still the same temptation that we know of from the third chapter of Genesis though in one sense more deep-rooted than ever. A time of great trial but also of great hope. For just such a time as this we have been given the sign: Christ, Sign of Contradiction. And the woman clothed with the sun 'a great sign in the heavens'."

This is the man the Cardinals chose in 1978 to be the Supreme Pastor of the Church. Catholics, other Christians and all men of good will who look for vision in today's world will find nourishment, I believe, in this book. The thoughts, the faith, and the serene courage of the new Pope, John Paul II, will help Christians to deepen their own faith, give them the courage to live it and the enthusiasm to share it.

BASIL HUME
Archbishop of Westminster

FOREWORD
TO THE ITALIAN EDITION

Cardinal Karol Wojtyla, Archbishop Metropolitan of Cracow, was called upon by our Holy Father Pope Paul VI to preach the word of life to the Vicar of Christ and his closest collaborators in the Vatican.

With a tinge of apprehensiveness, but with obedience and trust in the Holy Spirit, the Bishop of Cracow accepted this charge which did him such honour. To fulfil it he brought together his faith, his commitment to fervent prayer and all that he has inherited from his experience as a pastor. Richly endowed with all these gifts, he sought to carry out his task with the optimism of a strong Christian and the simplicity of a son of that nation which is accustomed to saying "Yes" only to God, to the Church of Christ and to his Mother.

This "Yes" – free of all hesitation – is the distinguishing mark of the talks delivered in the Vatican. Bishop Karol carried the "Yes" from the altar of St Stanislaus, Bishop and Martyr, whose relics are preserved in the historic shrine of Wawel, and brought the Good News with Franciscan humility and deep charity. His lively faith, deepened by study, meditation and prayer, and far removed from all professional dialectic, has released in him an apostolic fervour that today more than ever is the indispensable prerequisite for "renewing the face of the earth".

To confess openly that only Christ "is set for the fall and the rising of many" (Lk 2,34), to adhere to him and place all one's trust in him, is to open the door to this renewal.

That is the task which Cardinal Karol set himself in these addresses, given in the Matilda Chapel in the presence of the Holy Father. His gaze is on the "sign" whom the world contradicts. But he views with serenity this contradiction hurled at Christ by the world, because he knows that "in none other is salvation to be found". The human family may wander far from Christ, but then, weary of exploring blind alleys, it will come back to him with renewed hope.

The "sign" perceived by Simeon is "the blessed fruit of the womb" of the Mother of God; she too is visible to the world as a "great sign in the heavens" (Rev 12,1): "a woman clothed with sunlight". The world does battle with the Son and with his Mother. That is why she remains ever-present in the mystery of Christ and of the Church.

Calling to mind this hope throughout the Vatican retreat, the Bishop of Cracow offered the Holy Father and his collaborators a faithful and invaluable preaching of the word, envisaging "a new Advent for the Church and for humanity, a time of great trial but also of great hope".

STEFAN CARDINAL WYSZYNSKI
Primate of Poland

SIGN OF
CONTRADICTION

I.

Introductory address

1. *Homage and greetings*

> "May God grant me to speak of him as I would wish
> and shape thoughts worthy of the gifts bestowed upon
>   me,
> since he is the guide of wisdom... .
> We and our thoughts are indeed in his hand,
> our understanding too, and all our skill".
>
> (Wis 7,15–16)

Holy Father! At the start of this retreat which I have the honour to preach before you and your illustrious collaborators, I would like to express my deeply respectful homage and love for your person. I must, however, say at once that this tribute comes not from me alone. It is paid to you by all those with whom I am particularly closely linked, and who by their remembrance, their prayers and their sacrifices have promised their spiritual support for my humble service of the word during these days of retreat, not only to me but also to all my illustrious hearers – first to you, Holy Father, and then to the Lords Cardinals of the Holy Roman Church, the Most Reverend Archbishops, the Bishops and the beloved brethren in the priesthood.

We know full well that the prayer of the whole Church, today and always, focusses on the person of Paul, just as when the Church was very young its prayer focussed on the person of Peter (Acts 12,12–17).

In the days that lie ahead we shall have particularly with us the prayer of the Church in Poland, from which I bring greetings expressing the deepest communion in faith, hope and love – an invisible foundation but one which never fails to bind us to the successor of Peter.

In a special way I bring here the heart of the Church of Cracow, of which the Holy Spirit (cf Acts 20,28) – through your will, Holy Father – has made me Bishop and pastor.

With the homage of the ancient Church of Cracow – which is now celebrating the ninth centenary of the pastorate of St Stanislaus in that see – and in the name of God, and under the protection of the Immaculate Virgin, Mother of the Church, honoured by us as the Black Madonna of Czestochowa, of St Joseph, of the holy Apostles Peter and Paul and of our patron saints, I now – in accordance with your wish, Holy Father – begin this lenten retreat.

2. *Psalm 139 (138)*

> "Lord, you scrutinise and know me,
> if I sit or if I stand, you know it:
> you discern my thoughts from afar.
> You watch my every step
> and all my ways are familiar to you.
> Before a word reaches my tongue
> you know it, Lord, to the full.
> Behind me and before me you hold me in check
> and upon me you place your hand.
> Such knowledge is too wonderful for me,
> too sublime, and I cannot comprehend it.
> Where can I go to be distant from your spirit?
> Where flee from your presence?
>
> (Ps 139 (138), 1–7)

These words of the Psalmist come to our lips when we set about defining the very nature and meaning of a retreat. They are wonderfully expressive of a particular need of the human spirit to get as close as possible to God and to be penetrated by his Spirit. The Psalmist says: "Where can I go to be distant from your Spirit? Where flee from your presence?" But for us a retreat is a move in entirely the opposite direction: we want to get closer, we want the Lord to reach into our inmost hearts with his light, his presence and his grace. We set out towards him and our desire is to meet him in the days ahead. We wish to live this meeting to the full, deep within our being, human but at all times permeated with the divine presence. "You scrutinise and know me ... You discern my thoughts from afar ... Behind me and before me you hold me in check and upon me you place your hand."

A retreat does not consist only of a planned series of actions, addresses, prayer, spiritual concentration in an atmosphere of silence. Within all these things – and even further within our own being – it acts as an "urge" impelling us towards God. Sometimes difficulties weaken this "urge" when our day-to-day duties lack any religious content of their own. But when all that we do each day has a specifically religious reference, that is to say when our whole life is one of faith, hope, love, prayer and silence, a consecrated life always bound up with the Eucharist, then the "urge" towards God springs from integration of our being with our activity. A retreat is a case in point: even though it entails hard work and effort, its dominant motive is self-discovery through the search for spiritual well-being. So it is as if there were an opening-up of that inner space of human existence in which we can rejoice in the fact that "the Lord is close at hand" (Phil 4,5). We become conscious of his presence and activity in the world, in ourselves, in salvation history (cf Acts 17,18). So we feel the desire to enter as deeply as we can into the ambit of God's thoughts and purposes:

> "How fathomless to me are your purposes,
> and how vast is their span!
> Were I to count them, they are more than the sand,
> and at my waking I am still in your presence".

(Ps 139 (138), 17–18)

"O the depth of the riches, the wisdom and the knowledge
of God", writes the Apostle. Indeed: "Who has ever known
the mind of the Lord? Or who has been his counsellor?"
(Rom 11,33–34). Always we embark on a retreat with a
great desire to "enter into God": to enter as far as the
limitations of our human nature allow. "Deus, noverim Te!",
says St Augustine.[1] And although by this time we have long
since been meeting the Lord in prayer, although we seek to
serve him and work for the coming of his kingdom, nevertheless whenever we embark on a retreat we do so with an
implicit desire and a trustful expectation that he will allow us
to "enter into himself" even more. And so, like Moses (cf
Ex 3,5), in spirit we remove the shoes from our feet, on the
threshold of the inner sanctuary that each of us must become
as we meet the Lord.

Our retreat is also the period in which we confide in God
in a quite distinctive manner. Not for us some experiment
with knowledge, such as those of the scientist in his
laboratory and the thinker in his solitary questionings. For us
there is going to be a meeting with the living Truth and the
living Love. To this meeting we are bringing our lives, our
selves, concealing nothing, conveying everything, opening our
inmost being to him who "scrutinises and knows us"; and
with the Psalmist we say:

"Examine me, O God, and know my heart,
put me to the test and know my thoughts,
see if I have chosen any way of idolatry
and guide me along the age-old path".

(Ps 139 (138), 23–24)

The way to the great encounter – of which a retreat is the
external manifestation and at the same time the most
important stage – leads towards God but also towards man.
Humanity has a part to play by virtue of the principle of
exchange, a wonderful exchange that is possible only
between man and God, because an exchange of God for man
did once take place: "Admirabile commercium" (Liturgy of

the hours, Ant. 1.i). This is my aim when I open myself to the Lord, placing myself before him in all inner truth and pleading: "Examine me, Lord!" A little bit like a sick man talking to his doctor. "Examine my heart!" My very heart, which is not only an organ of central importance but also the vital test of man's effectiveness, of man who is both flesh and spirit. But not merely: "Examine me, Lord!" I am not asking only for a diagnosis, but rather for the application of a sort of "divine expertise". I am asking: "Put me to the test!" This testing is not only the beginning of knowing. In a sense it constitutes fulness of knowing, as well as being the groundwork for further, more searching checks. The Psalmist seeks, and we seek with him, to become the object of this "divine expertise". Therein lies the fulness of spiritual experience in a retreat.

"Put me to the test, Lord, and know my anxieties!" Human existence is – wrote Martin Heidegger[2] – an anxiety in itself. The deepest and noblest of all anxieties, and the one most in keeping with the atmosphere of a retreat, is precisely the one the Psalmist points to: "See if I have chosen any way of idolatry and guide me along the age-old path." Augustine's "noverim me", together with his "noverim Te", marks out the fundamental structure of the retreat, the true nature of that particular "urge" which each of us feels and which is the work of that unseen Mover – "Deus absconditus" (Is 45,15) – to whom we turn so often: "Sine Tuo Numine nihil est in homine, nihil est innoxium. ..."

At this time of year the Church in Poland organises numerous retreats: not only the customary parish ones during Lent but also retreats arranged specifically for young people – who make no secret of their need for them. Often the numbers wishing to attend exceed our very modest organisational potential – as has been the case this year in my own archdiocese with students in their final year at school. Only two thousand places were available, but the number of applications was far greater than that. It is just the same in the summer, in the Oases movement. I frequently talk to these youngsters, and I find it most interesting to listen to their experiences which – it must be said – all gravitate around one fundamental conclusion: for them their retreat is first and foremost an experience of meeting God, of rediscovering God and themselves, an experience that brings with it fresh discovery of the meaning of life. And these youngsters of whom I am speaking very often emerge from a "great darkness" surrounding them, the darkness devised by the whole of the secularising, anti-religious system of state education.

> "I think to myself: at least the darkness will cover me
> and night will close in around me.
> But even the darkness is light for you
> and night is as brilliant as day".
>
> (Ps 139 (138), 11–12)

Though surrounded by that darkness, these young people journey on, trusting in God's presence, trusting in the meaning of this world, trusting in the beauty of creation which they seek to know and understand as they wend their way through forests and across mountain ranges.

> "I shall take the wings of daybreak,
> and dwell at the uttermost bounds of the sea.
> Even there your hand still leads me
> your right hand holds me fast ...".
>
> (Ps 139 (138), 9–10)

3. *The Hymn of Simeon*

Holy Father, venerable brethren!

We come now to the evening office. The whole Church is reciting the last part of the liturgy of the hours, Compline. In it we are reminded each day of the words of that aged Jew called Simeon who, on seeing the child Jesus in the arms of his mother on the threshold of the temple, said – quite unexpectedly for all around him and perhaps also for himself:

"Now, O Lord, let your servant depart in peace, in accordance with your word; for my eyes have gazed upon the saviour whom you have prepared for all peoples to see, a light that shines for the gentiles and the glory of your people Israel" (Lk 2,29–32).

"My eyes have gazed upon the light ...". With these words we habitually end our day's work, thinking about the light that he is for us too. And we give thanks, and express our delight at being able to walk in that light, at being able to see our lives and those of others in that light, able always to shape life anew in that light, to spare no effort in serving it and to live for it alone.

Today too we give thanks, because we are confident that our retreat will enable us to enter the ever brighter ambit of the light which shone for the eyes of Simeon.

All the same, as we recite the words of Simeon's hymn we cannot lose sight of those with which he then addressed the child's mother:

"Behold, he is set for the fall and the rising of many in Israel, and as a sign of contradiction; and for your part a sword will pierce your soul, so that the thoughts of many hearts may be laid bare" (Lk 2,34–35).

Although we do not recite them during Compline, I have linked these words of Simeon's with his wonderful prophetic hymn; and I have done so because I want them to stand out in relief. I see them as the connecting thread of all our meditations. Don't these words, spoken at the sight of the little child, bring together in a wonderful synthesis all that has the most profound impact on us and unceasingly perturbs us? Are they not a sign of our own times, or at least the key to understanding the various symptoms displayed by modern life, symptoms with which the second Vatican Council concerned itself, and the Synod of Bishops too, and which are of continual concern to the Holy See and all the bishops together with the People of God? Might not these words be a distinctive definition of Christ and of his Church? "The sign of contradiction". It should not be overlooked that immediately after the "sign of contradiction" Simeon turns directly to the mother and her heart, linking the contradiction – which refers to the Son – with the inner experience of the mother: "For your part a sword will pierce your soul". Simeon ends his prophetic utterance with a saying that is enigmatic and yet full of meaning: "... so that the thoughts of many hearts may be laid bare".

In the days of retreat ahead of us we shall try to bring ourselves face to face with all these words, face to face with the truth they contain. And may the "light that shines for the gentiles" be with us in this spiritual undertaking of ours. May this light give us strength and make us capable of accepting and loving the whole truth of Christ, of loving it all the more as the world all the more contradicts it.

Notes

1. St Augustine, *Soliloquiorum libri duo*, II–I, 1.
2. M. Heidegger, *Sein und Zeit*, Tübingen 1967[11].

II.

God of infinite majesty

1. *"Itinerarium mentis in Deum"*

"Deus immensae maiestatis". This is the God to whom I would like to direct attention in this present meditation. This is the God before whom we need to echo the words of the prophet Jeremiah: "Alas, Lord God, see, I do not know how to speak ..." (Jer 1,6). These are the words we must remember every time we take to the road that leads man's thought to God.

We need to recognise all the shortcomings, all the inadequacies of human thought concerning God. And we also need to take account of all the effort called for by the *itinerarium*.

> "Lord, you scrutinise and know me...
> Behind me and before me you hold me in check...
> For you formed my inmost parts,
> you knit me together in my mother's womb.
> I give you thanks, for in a wondrous way I was made,
> marvellous are your works, and well I know it"
> (Ps 139 (138), 1–14)

The *itinerarium mentis in Deum* – as St Bonaventure called it – emerges from deep within man, from within all created things and from acute analysis of the universe. It can take definite shape within the context of any of the various types and levels of our knowledge of the cosmos: from the earliest and most primitive to the present-day scientific, which is busy exploring the world with wonderful precision. This is true of such knowledge whatever the school of

thought, whether it be dependent on the cosmology of
Aristotle, the astronomy of Ptolemy or that of Copernicus,
the physics of Newton or that of Einstein, and so on.

Let us hear what the book of Wisdom has to say: "Fools,
for sure, by nature are men who know nothing of God"
(Wis 13,1). The Psalmist speaks even more clearly: "The fool
says in his heart: 'There is no God'..." (Ps 53(52),2).

The book of Wisdom goes on to say: "from the good
things that are visible they have failed to know Him-who-is;
nor, while studying his works, have they recognised the
craftsman ... for from the grandeur and beauty of created
things come perception of their creator" (Wis 13,1–5).

The *itinerarium mentis in Deum* derivable from the book
of Wisdom is by no means a thing of the distant past,
superseded. In substance, though in a developed form, it is
still to be found in the letter to the Romans; and such an
itinerarium will always be for man a continual summons and
a continual challenge. St Paul writes: "Ever since the
creation of the world, his invisible perfections – his everlasting power, his divinity – have been clearly perceptible
from the things he has made; so they have no excuse ..."
(Rom 1,20). Who has no excuse? Those "who unjustly keep
the truth imprisoned" (Rom 1,18): that is the context of St
Paul's assertion.

Perhaps we have now become more cautious in our
statements and judgments. We would certainly have difficulty nowadays in pronouncing the sentence on fools that we
find in the book of Wisdom and St Paul's letter. All the same
those words do stand where they do. And so we have to ask
ourselves: if they survive in holy scripture almost like a relic
of a bygone age – that primitive, non-scientific, somewhat
ingenuous age which was ignorant of all the richness and
complexity of the world's structure, and was incapable of
identifying secondary causes and consequently of recognising
the autonomy of created things – might that not be because
for men of that age all things did refer directly to the
ultimate cause, the Creator himself?

2. *Anti-itinerary*

No matter how we choose to confront this problem, one thing seems certain: the difficulties and objections, the philosophical and epistemological concepts which were clear for the first Vatican Council to see have become even more formidable in this era of the second Vatican Council. The old difficulties nurtured by idealism, rationalism and semi-rationalism – or on the other hand fed by materialistic empiricism and hedonism, like rigid systems and laws that brook no argument – have by this time been replaced by new philosophical and epistemological concepts. And these seem even more bent on destroying the aims of human knowledge. Now not only God and the whole spiritual order are under threat but also, in one sense, man himself and the world around him. Structuralism, for instance, goes much further than agnosticism or even positivism. Against the background of this bewildering development in thought, which calls in question thought itself and casts doubt on the subject and the very meaning of knowledge, a most peculiar theology has emerged: the theology of the death of God. This asserts that God died out of human thought as human thought underwent a process of self-criticism. The theology of the death of God reflects a tragic crisis in present-day thought, even though in one way the thinkers of today can take a genuine pride in the enormous advances that have been made in knowledge of the world in its macro and micro dimensions. The sheer efficiency of this present-day knowledge is breathtaking, sometimes even frightening, especially when one considers the speed and acceleration of its progress, particularly in the field of the application of science to technology. But now, at a time when man has "subdued the earth" (Gen 1,28; Ps 8,6–9) to a degree never before known – at least as far as we can judge – now, when he has extended so very far the "horizontal" thread of his knowledge, what strikes one most forcibly is a lack of balance in relation to the "vertical" component of that knowledge.

Present-day man – one could say – does not think things through to the end, does not seek the fundamental reasons why, looks for no foothold in knowledge of him whom the book of Wisdom proclaims as the Creator. The thinkers of antiquity however, as they followed the connecting thread of their analysis of reality, being and goodness, spoke of the Prime Mover or of the supreme Idea of the Good. And today it often occurs to us to wonder whether the truth that lay beneath that thought and that knowledge really is superseded, outdated; whether it is true that by now there is nothing left of the road which used to lead the human mind almost spontaneously from the visible world to God. Something must have happened: has human knowledge perhaps chosen to branch off laterally along a minor road, abandoning the main trunk routes?

I have had a number of opportunities to discuss these and similar matters with scientists, especially physicists, who today constitute a group *sui generis* of "experts on the subject". I remember a long discussion with one of them, an eminent scholar and a man of great honesty, who said to me: "From the point of view of my own science and its method, I am an atheist, and if you people argue from the starting-point of the proofs of the existence of God, I do not accept them, because as a scientist I cannot see any grounds for them". But that same man once wrote to me in all sincerity: "Every time I find myself confronted with the grandeur of nature, of the mountain ranges, I feel that God exists!" We might detect here an echo from the book of Wisdom: "The author of beauty created them. And if what has so impressed men is their strength and their force, let them understand from these things how much more powerful is he who formed them ..." (Wis 13,3–4).

St Thomas makes a very precise distinction between empirical knowledge and wisdom. When the author of the book of Wisdom calls those who do not know God "fools", the knowledge he has in mind is much more than empirical: it is the sort of knowledge that is nothing less than wisdom.

Wisdom always seeks the fundamental reasons why, asserts the philosopher, and he sees in metaphysics the purest expression of wisdom. The Psalmist sang: "The fear of God is the beginning of wisdom" (Ps 111 (110),10). The Apostle in his turn wrote: "Mere knowledge puffs up, whereas charity builds up" (1 Cor 8,1). These are different aspects of the same thing which – as can be seen – is not only intellectual but also moral.

Then there is, too, the problem of the "divinisation" of matter, which the author of the book of Wisdom expressed in terminology typical of his time: "fire and wind, the swift air, the starry vault, the turbulent waters, heaven's luminaries, these they believed to be gods, rulers of the world". The modern mind, thanks to Christianity, is free of the temptation to divinise the forces of nature. But at the same time philosophical and theoretical materialism – and every-day materialism too – are both doing their best to turn matter into an absolute in human thought. I can remember several publications, typical of the early postwar years in Poland, in which Catholic intellectuals in argument with Marxists demonstrated that matter cannot have the character of an absolute. Arguments of that type have now died down: attention is now concentrated on the anthro-pological problem, although the *weltanschauung* and the marxist system go on asserting that matter constitutes the be-all and end-all of man, his beginning and his end, the fulness of the reality which completely defines the purpose of his existence as an individual.

3. *Existence and the person*

The *itinerarium mentis in Deum* is a route to be taken by man's thought, or rather by the whole man. Thus it is *itinerarium hominis.* By following this route man reaches his own inner space. The route emerges from the depths of created things and from man's own inmost being, and against the background of the universe man sees himself to be

relative and contingent, his existence fragile and his limits
many. "You formed my inmost parts, you knit me together
in my mother's womb" (Ps 139(138),13). In those terms the
Bible expresses the truth about man as creature, man as a
being who is relative and contingent.

The creaturely state and the state of an *ens contingens* are
two different concepts but each directs human thought "ad
Deum". The key to the itinerary is the being in his existential
aspect, as in the thought of St Thomas and the thomists. The
being's contingency means his limitation, as distinct from his
existence. Of itself contingency points to the absolute, not
only as its opposite in the dialectical sense but also as the
real basis, the fundamental reason why, of any contingent
being; the absolute explains the existence of a world made up
of contingent beings, a world that is itself contingent and
relative. The Absolute is a necessary being, in the sense that
it is *"Ipsum Esse subsistens"*.

This metaphysical key to the understanding and interpretation of reality, with the Absolute as philosophical
correlate of God, has now undoubtedly lost its former
privileged position in philosophy. Nonetheless – as one of the
younger generation of Polish philosophers asserts[1] – post-
cartesian philosophy, though basically anthropocentric, has
not succeeded in detaching itself completely from the
problem of God. On the contrary, like phenomenology and
existentialism it is rich in christian inspiration. But the God
of this philosophy is no longer the *"Ipsum Esse subsistens"*:
the God of this philosophy is first and foremost a Person, the
divine "Thou" who permits the human "I" to take shape and
develop – as another Polish philosopher puts it[2]. In
Ratzinger's book entitled *An introduction to Christianity* we
find an important analysis of Exodus 3,14 – God's reply to
Moses who has asked for his true name. The words "I am
who I am", hitherto interpreted as the correlate of the
"Ipsum Esse subsistens", are seen by this German theologian
to convey revelation of the Person. According to him, God

used those words to define himself as the fulness of personal Being.

In present-day thought there is a great tension between denial and affirmation of God. In saying "present-day thought" we were referring to its "objectivisation" in philosophical systems and metaphysical reflection. Now we have to go a step further and ask ourselves: what impression does the truth of God leave on the mind of the ordinary man, the non-philosopher? This question frequently crops up in sociological research. The replies to it usually show that this fundamental religious truth still retains a right of citizenship in the ambit of the ordinary man's knowledge, and in that of his inner convictions.

It is characteristic of this fundamental religious truth that it survives even in conditions of systematic and planned denial of God. I shall never forget the impression left with me by a Russian soldier in 1945. The war was only just over. A conscript knocked at the door of the Cracow seminary. When I asked "What is it you want?" he replied that he wished to enter the seminary. Our conversation went on for a long time. Even though he never in fact entered (incidentally he was far from clear in his mind about what a seminary really is) our meeting taught me, personally, one great truth: how wonderfully God succeeds in penetrating the human mind even in the extremely unfavourable conditions of systematic denial of him. In the whole of his adult life that man had scarcely ever gone inside a church. At school, and then later at work, he had continually heard people asserting "There is no God!" And in spite of all that he said more than once: "But I always knew that God exists ... and now I would like to learn something about him ...".

4. *The language of silence*

The *itinerarium mentis in Deum* emerges from the depths of created things and from a man's inmost being. The modern mentality as it makes its way finds its support in human experience, and in affirmation of the transcendence of the human person. Man goes beyond himself, man must go beyond himself. The tragedy of atheistic humanism – so brilliantly analysed by Père De Lubac[3] – is that it strips man of his transcendental character, destroying his ultimate significance as a person. Man goes beyond himself by reaching out towards God, and thus progresses beyond the limits imposed on him by created things, by space and time, by his own contingency. The transcendence of the person is closely bound up with responsiveness to the one who himself is the touchstone for all our judgments concerning being, goodness, truth and beauty. It is bound up with responsiveness to the one who is nevertheless totally Other, because he is infinite.

The concept of infinity is not unknown to man. He makes use of it in his scientific work, in mathematics for instance. So there certainly is room in him, in his intellectual understanding, for him who is infinite, the God of boundless majesty, the one to whom holy scripture and the Church bear witness saying: "Holy, holy, holy, God of the universe, heaven and earth are full of your glory!". This God is professed in his silence by the Trappist or the Camaldolite. It is to him that the desert Bedouin turns at his hour for prayer. And perhaps the Buddhist too, wrapt in contemplation as he purifies his thought, preparing the way to Nirvana. God in his absolute transcendence, God who transcends absolutely the whole of creation, all that is visible and comprehensible.

During its first session the Synod of Bishops considered among other things the problem of atheism. The monks of the contemplative orders had sent to the Synod a most characteristic letter[4] expressing their understanding of the attitude of present-day atheists when they considered it in the light of their own experience, that is to say as men of faith, prayer and total dedication to God but who, despite all that, are not exempt from darkness of the spirit and the senses. One of the paradoxes of the God of infinite majesty, the transcendent God!

St John of the Cross has left us a beautiful testimony to such an experience:

> "To attain to this which you know not
> you must pass through that which you know not.
> To attain to this which you possess not
> you must pass through that which you possess not.
> To attain to this which you are not
> you must pass through that which you are not".

The Church of the living God gathers together all men, who in one way or another share this marvellous transcendence of the human spirit. And all of them know that nobody except the God of infinite majesty can satisfy their deepest longings (cf *Gaudium et spes*, n.41).

This transcendence of the human person manifests itself in the prayer of faith, but from time to time in profound silence too. This silence, which sometimes seems to separate man from God, is nonetheless a special manifestation of the vital bond linking God and the human spirit.

The Church of our day has become particularly conscious of this truth; and it was in the light of this truth that the Church succeeded, during the second Vatican Council, in re-defining her own nature.

Notes

1. Cf J. Tischner, *The world of human hope*, Cracow 1975.
2. M. Jaworski, *Man and God. Reflections on the connection between the human person and God and the problem of atheism*, in 'Logos i Ethos', Cracow 1971.
3. H. De Lubac, *Athéisme et sens de l'homme*, Paris 1969.
4. Cf G. Caprile, *Il Sinodo dei Vescovi*, Rome 1968.

III.

God of the covenant

---

1. *The first and fundamental covenant*

In this meditation let us turn our minds afresh towards God as the Lord of infinite majesty who chose to become for us the God of the covenant as well.

Here are the words of the fourth eucharistic prayer:

> "We praise you, Father, holy one,
> for your greatness:
> you made all things with wisdom and love;
> you formed man in your own likeness,
> to his hands you entrusted the universe
> so that in obedience to you, his creator,
> he might exercise dominion over the whole created
> world".
>
> (Roman Missal)

Not for nothing does the fourth eucharistic prayer place in the forefront that age-old covenant with God the Creator which is so concisely described in the first three chapters of the book of Genesis. The prayer next refers briefly to the many other covenants which God went on to offer to men in preparation for the final one which he offered to the whole of humanity in the incarnation of his only Son. Many considerations prompt us, particularly in our own day, to meditate upon that first covenant offered to man – to our humanity, one could well say – in the first man: that "first Adam". He was the "primus homo de terra, terrenus"; and the first covenant, received by him as part of the mystery of the divine plan, was "complemented" in the second covenant, when "God loved the world so much that he sacrificed his only-begotten Son" (Jn 3,16): "secundus homo de coelo, coelestis" (1 Cor 15,45–49; Rom 5,11–16).

2. *The motive for creation and the motive for the covenant*

Let us pause to consider the main features of the covenant as outlined in the book of Genesis and the letters of St Paul. The fundamental problem requiring clarification is this: why does the God of infinite majesty, the Absolute, the master of the created world, become a God of the covenant? St John's answer is: "He loved the world so much". That same love is to be found again in the pages of Genesis. Love always wills the good, and wills it disinterestedly: "love is kind", says the Apostle Paul (1 Cor 13,4). And so love creates the good. When we open the book of Genesis we straightaway light upon this truth: "And God said: 'Let all the waters that are under heaven come together in one place, and let the dry land appear (1,9). ... Let the earth bring forth grasses, plants to yield seed and trees to bear fruit, that each may give produce according to its kind' (1, 11). ... And God saw that it was good" (1,12). The inspired author ends his account with: "And God saw all that he had made; and behold, it was very good" (1,31).

This is why at every stage in the development of human thought, reflection upon the ontology of the universe, reflection upon being, must always move in step with reflection upon the axiology of the world, reflection upon the good and its values. Such is the structure of the created world; and the human mind, no matter what premiss it starts from, will always in the final analysis confirm in one way or another the truth of creation, the truth implicit in the first chapter of Genesis.

Even when man, as he reflects on the world, concentrates solely on its economic processes when he considers the functions of economic value and super-value, he will – if he remains on a realistic plane in his thinking and reasoning –

find himself on the plane and the level indicated in the first chapter of Genesis.

"And God saw that it was good". This divine "seeing" is in every way primary, because it creates being and good and also ensures their continuance within time: *conservatio est continua creatio*. Human seeing and human doing are always secondary because they are always concerned with something already provided; they always encounter pre-constituted being and value.

The contingent being is not a necessary being. The created world is not an absolute. But the goodness of the created world – created contingent and thus non-necessary – shows us that the motive for creation is love. Love is the motive for creation and, consequently, love is the motive for the covenant. One might say that this love is the root from which stem both the eternal plan of salvation, in the form of concrete expression of God's love for man, and the personal transcendence of man in relation to the whole of the created world.

Already in the first chapter of Genesis and the first biblical description of creation – which in the light of literary criticism would appear to have been written later than the second in the same book – we find that God-Elohim "created man in his own image, in the image of God he created him; male and female he created them" (Gen 1,27).

The description we find in the second chapter, the older one, seems to be closer to the modern trend towards biological evolutionism, that of Père Teilhard de Chardin for instance. "And the Lord God formed man from the dust of the earth and breathed into his nostrils a breath of life; and man became a living being" (Gen 2,7).

Then follows the detailed description of the creation of woman and the establishment of the first community of human persons, called by Vatican II "communio personarum" (*Gaudium et spes*, n.12).

To a certain extent the covenant – the primordial one – is instituted together with creation. It stems from the same

basic motive, disinterested love, that love which St Thomas
Aquinas was to express in philosophico-theological terms as:
bonum est diffusivum sui.[1] It is indeed so: the God of infinite
majesty – *Ipsum esse subsistens*[2] – distributes in varying
degrees of perfection the good of existence, and spreads it as
he effects creation; spreads it because he is not only
omnipotence but also love.

In this process of creation – which, regarded from the
angle of its external effects, takes the form of evolution of
the universe – the time comes for the creation of man. He
who, as *Ipsum esse subsistens*, is the fulness of personal being
takes yet another step forward along the way mapped out by
the principle *bonum est diffusivum sui*, and in creating
human beings "in his own image" – that is to say endowed
with transcendence and a spiritual character – offers these
beings, mankind, his covenant. From being the God of
creation he becomes the God of the covenant. This comes
about in accordance with the logic which, from the
beginning, governs the whole work of creation. It is a logic of
love, which can perhaps be thought of as the logic Pascal
spoke of: "le coeur a ses raisons". Yes, "le coeur" – the
heart! Throughout the description in Genesis the heart can
be heard beating. We have before us not a great builder of
the world, a demiurge: we stand in the presence of the great
heart!

No cosmogony, no philosophical cosmology of the past, no
cosmological theory of the present-day can express a truth
like this truth. We can find it only in the inspired pages of
Genesis: revelation of the love that pervades the whole earth
to its very core, revelation of the Fatherhood which gives
creation its full meaning, together with the covenant which
gives rise to the creation of man in the image of God.

3. *The structure of the covenant*

One of the essential elements of this covenant is man's
dominion over the earth: "have mastery over the fish of the

sea, the birds of heaven, the animals and the whole earth" (Gen 1,26). Let us pause to consider this concept. This dominion extends over all that man little by little succeeds in deriving from the earth as he continually discovers, thanks to his intelligence, new values and new potential. But even when – as in our day – man reaches the moon, he can do this only by virtue of the first covenant, from which and thanks to which he received the prerogative of dominion.

Yet this is not the sole element of the covenant; there are many besides. The covenant springs from the great heart, from God's love for man. At the same time it is built on truth, rooted in what is real, that is to say: true.[3] God gave man this commandment: "You may eat freely of every tree in the garden: but of the tree of the knowledge of good and evil you must not eat, for the day you eat of it you will surely die" (Gen 2,16–17). Thus from the very dawn of history man is faced with a tree: the tree of the knowledge of good and evil, the tree which is a symbol of his human nature in that it is a sign of the limits implicit in his creaturely state and, at the same time, the frontier which development of the human person may not cross. The human person created in the image of God is not set "beyond the confines of good and evil", as Nietzsche and other propounders of the absolute autonomy of man would have it.

Here is the tree of the knowledge of good and evil: a symbol of being and value, the first and most fundamental of all the restrictive situations now studied by existentialist philosophy. And the tree of the knowledge of good and evil is linked symbolically with the tree of life (cf Gen 2,9). The covenant we are now discussing was a gift of grace on God's part, and on the part of man – man and woman – it was a state of primitive righteousness and happiness. It is difficult to provide a detailed analysis of a state of that kind. It is well known to be one of the most interesting of theological subjects. But that is not all.

A non-Catholic philosopher once said to me: "You know – I just can't stop myself reading and re-reading and thinking

over the first three chapters of Genesis". And indeed it seems
to me that unless one does so reflect upon that fundamental
ensemble of facts and situations it becomes extremely
difficult – if not impossible – to understand man and the
world. It may sound a trifle strange, but I think it is true,
that today one cannot understand either Sartre or Marx
without having first read and pondered very deeply the first
three chapters of Genesis. These are the key to understanding the world of today, both its roots and its extremely
radical – and therefore dramatic – affirmations and denials.
We shall discuss the denials in the next meditation.

It should be borne in mind that careful study of that first
covenant – and, at the same time, of the first portrayal of the
God of the covenant – is central to all reflection on the
Church-world relationship. As was the case during the
second Vatican Council, which brought the Constitution on
the Church to completion by adding to it the Constitution on
the Church in the World of Today. That was no accident.

Rather it was a logical consequence of the work of the
Council, which wanted to delineate precisely the relationship
between the Church and the world of today. To do that it
was necessary to go right back to the fundamental reality of
creation – of the world and of man – and to the first
covenant, which is the foundation for the definitive covenant
offered by God to humanity in Jesus Christ. The Church is,
precisely, a sign of that covenant.

At much the same time the Holy Father issued his first
encyclical, which set out to deepen awareness of the Church
and which is the basis for all dialogue with the world of
today. It is a dialogue of salvation, and its beginnings have to
be sought in the covenant, that is to say in that fundamental
first dialogue between God and man. It seems to me that
nowadays we are sorely in need of a correct understanding of
that first dialogue and that first covenant. Why? Perhaps
because humanity as a whole is uncovering and clarifying
with ever greater thoroughness the origins of man's existence
on earth. And perhaps, too, because today we are on the

threshold of a new eschatology. And eschatology can be fully understood only when it goes right back to the beginnings, to the most fundamental problems within which lie, implicit but hidden, the outlines of the ultimate truths, eschatological truths. Something like an embryo, containing all that will in time make up the full-grown person.

4. *Towards the covenant in all its fulness*

"Again and again you offered mankind your covenant", says the eucharistic prayer. We know very well which covenants it refers to. Among the ones we learn of in Genesis, the one offered to Abraham merits particular attention. This is a covenant offered to man at the level of his humanity, as was the case with the first: a covenant offered to the entire people which was to descend from Abraham. "I am El Shaddai; walk in my presence and be perfect. I shall establish my pact between me and you, and I shall multiply you hugely" (Gen 17,1–2). To begin with this was more a pact with a family or clan than with a people. It acquired the dimension of a covenant with an entire people in consequence of Moses. And this covenant with a family and a people points the way to the conclusive covenant with man, with humanity, in the Son of God. This is the definitive dimension of the covenant. "The God and Father of our Lord Jesus Christ" (2 Cor 1,3), writes the Apostle; really "Father"! With the full revelation of the divine Fatherhood comes full and far-reaching confirmation of the covenant made when man was created. That covenant, shattered once by original sin, is to be rebuilt by redemption, with foundations that go deeper still and dimensions even vaster. "Happy fault, which gained for us so great a redeemer" *(Easter proclamation)*. The fourth eucharistic prayer develops the theme of the God of the covenant with these words:

"Father, holy one, you loved the world so much that you sent us, in the fulness of time, your only Son to be our Saviour.

He became man through the working of the Holy Spirit and was born of the Virgin Mary. ... And that we might live no longer for ourselves but for him who died and rose again for us, you sent us, Father, the Holy Spirit, first gift to those who believe, to perfect his work on earth and bring us the fulness of grace."

Here is the definitive form of the covenant. Here is the Fatherhood, which is God's deepest mystery and at the same time God's greatest revelation of himself, in the Son: the Son in whom he can himself be discerned: "He who has seen me has seen the Father" (Jn 14,9).

The Church, conscious of the depth of meaning of this covenant, was to say of herself in the second Vatican Council that she is "in Christ a kind of sacrament or sign and instrument of intimate unity with God and of the unity of all mankind" (*Lumen gentium*, n.1). All men are embraced by this sacrament of unity. Let us ponder its depth and its potentialities; let us, especially, remember it – we who, as we daily celebrate the Eucharist, profess and proclaim this "new and everlasting covenant". When we receive God in the Eucharist, it is he who receives us! The God of infinite majesty is very close to us. In this wonderful sacrament he allows us to touch him, to eat him: he welcomes each one of us, helps us to our feet again and again, and assures us of our great worth.

Truly, the God of the covenant is the God of infinite majesty!

Notes

1. *Sum. Theol.* I, q.5, a.4, ad 2.
2. *Sum. Theol.* II–I, q.3, a.2, ad 3.
3. Cf Blaise Pascal, *Pensées*, 272.

IV.

The ways of denial

1. *The second Vatican Council on atheism*

In today's meditation we are going to try to explore, as far as is possible, the ways of denial of God.

In *Gaudium et spes* the second Vatican Council provided a very perspicacious analysis of the changes in religious sensibility in the world of today. Then, in a short but succinct summing-up, it looked at the various phenomena that commonly fall under the general heading of "atheism".

After first outlining the psychological and moral changes typical of our age, the conciliar document says:

"Finally, even the spiritual life is influenced by these new situations. On the one hand a more acute critical sense is freeing religion from all magical conceptions of the world and from any surviving superstitions, and is increasingly insisting on a more personal and active adherence to the faith. As a result many people are attaining a sharper awareness of God. On the other hand growing numbers of people are, in practice, detaching themselves from religion. Unlike in former times, denial of God or of religion – or in practice doing without them – are no longer unusual and individual occurrences. Today it is quite often said that they are in fact called for by scientific progress and a new type of humanism. In many countries all this finds expression not only in the reasonings of philosophers; it has also made great inroads into the fields of literature, the arts, the interpretation of history and the human sciences, and even into civil law, with the result that many people have lost their bearings" (n. 7).

Elsewhere (n. 19) the Constitution says: "The term 'atheism' is here applied to phenomena which differ considerably from one another". It is in that article and the next that we find, as we have said, a most careful analysis of the various phenomena, in a text that is very concise but rich in content. After analysing atheism as an inner state of the human conscience, the document deals with atheism as a system.

For the time being, however, let us leave all that on one side and turn to the first chapters of Genesis. We must do this, because anyone wanting to get to the root of this problem of denial of God must start from a non-superficial analysis of that very first denial. So we have to go delving deeper than the reality of man: we have to delve into the reality of Satan. Quite obviously present-day anthropocentrism – even the christian and theological variety – will have little or nothing to do with it: we all remember the outcry when the Holy Father quite simply recalled the elementary truths of Church teaching on the subject.[1] The Sacred Congregation for the Doctrine of the Faith restated them in *The Christian Faith and the doctrine concerning Satan*.

2. *Analysing the original denial*

Satan, the evil spirit, is portrayed in Genesis as an already existing reality, already operating in the world. The biblical description of the creation of the universe is concerned only with visible reality, with the "earth" and the "heavens", components of the empirical cosmos; that description is silent concerning what is a non-empirical reality. All the same, even though Genesis does not explain the origins of Satan, the evil spirit, we can at once identify him with ease when he first puts in an appearance.

"The serpent was more cunning than all the wild animals that the Lord God had made" (Gen 3,1). So we start on the level of nature, within the framework of description of the empirical world. Immediately afterwards, however, comes the sentence which removes us from that level and takes us outside the empirical world: "He said to the woman: 'Did God really say: Do not eat the fruit of any of the trees in the garden?' The woman answered the serpent: 'We may eat of the trees in the garden, but as for the fruit of the tree in the middle of the garden God said: Do not eat it; indeed do not touch it or you will die.' But the serpent said to the woman: 'No, you will not die; God in fact knows that were you to eat it your eyes would open and you would become like God, acquiring knowledge of good and evil' " (Gen 3,1–5).

Man finds these words astonishing. The evil spirit is recognisable and identifiable not by means of some definition of his being but solely from the content of his words. Here, in the third chapter of Genesis, at the very beginning of the bible, it becomes clear that the history of mankind, and with it the history of the world with which man is united through the work of divine creation, will both be subject to rule by the Word and the anti-Word, the Gospel and the anti-Gospel. Until now we have been hearing the Word, which made itself evident in the straightforward assent of all created things, the work of God, and above all in the assent of man created in the image of God. Now let us see the route taken by the anti-Word.

It all begins with the first lie. This could be seen as an innocent piece of mistaken information; it could even be taken for a request for reliable information. The woman unhesitatingly corrects the faulty information, perhaps without sensing that this is merely an opening gambit, a prelude to what the "father of lies" is about to say to her. Here is what follows: first he calls in question God's veracity: "you will not die"; next he strikes at the heart of the covenant. The God of the covenant is made to look like a king jealous of his rule, an adversary of man whom man needs to resist, against whom man needs to rebel. Finally Satan spells out the temptation, for which his source is his own rebellion and denial: "Were you to eat it your eyes would open and you would become like God, acquiring knowledge of good and evil" (Gen 3,4–5).

When the father of lies approaches man he does not deny the existence of God; he does not deny God the existence and omnipotence to which creation bears witness; he aims straight at the God of the covenant.

Outright denial of God is not possible because his existence is too apparent in the created world, in man ... even in Satan himself. The Apostle James wrote: "even the demons believe in him, and tremble" (2, 19), showing that even they are incapable of denying God's existence and his sovereign power over all beings. But the truth about the God of the covenant, about the God who creates out of love, who in love offers humanity the covenant in Adam, who for love's sake puts to man requirements which have direct bearing on the truth of man's creaturely being – this is the truth that is destroyed in what Satan says. And the destruction is total.

That is what I mean by the anti-Word. But this anti-Word is at the same time made to relate closely to the Word. Did the Word say perhaps that man and woman have been created in the likeness of God? Well, declares Satan, "you will become like God, acquiring knowledge of good and evil". It is almost as if he were drawing the obvious conclusion, or at least a probable conclusion, from the Word itself: If you were created in the likeness of God, doesn't that include God-like knowledge of good and evil? Yet Satan is not merely the author of the false conclusion. He is determined to impose his own position, his own attitude to God. Man's "divinity" is of no importance to him whatsoever. The only thing that matters to him is to transmit to man his own rebellion, that is to say the attitude with which he – Satan – has identified himself and by which he has, in consequence, placed himself outside the truth; which means outside the law of dependence on the Creator. That is the message of his "non serviam" (Jer 2,20) which is the true antithesis of another self-revealing saying: Michael: "Who, like God ... ?" (Jude 9; Rev 12,7). And the subject in this "non serviam" became – according to tradition – the greatest of all created intelligences: "Daystar, son of Dawn" (cf Is 14,12).

Thus in those few sentences in Genesis the evil spirit made himself evident and disclosed his nature. The temptation offered by Satan goes beyond what was in fact accepted by the first humans, male and female. Yet even what was accepted was enough to point the direction in which later development of the temptation of mankind was to move.

What is so striking in the third chapter is the ontological and psychological accuracy of the biblical description. The woman does not accept the temptation in full: she accepts it only within the limits of her human conscience and freedom. Nonetheless, what she did accept was, unhappily, enough. Let us hear what the biblical text says: "Then the woman observed that the fruit on the tree was good to eat, pleasing to the eye and desirable for the knowledge it could give. So she plucked some of the fruit and ate it, and also gave some to her husband, and he too ate some of it. Then the eyes of both opened and they knew that they were naked" (Gen 3,6–7).

3. *The history of temptation of mankind*

Here we have the beginning, or better still the origins of temptation of mankind, the origins of a very long process that winds its devious way throughout history. Even in the apparent simplicity of the biblical description we cannot fail to be struck by the depth, and present-day relevance, of this problem. Satan does not achieve complete victory; that is to say he shows himself incapable of sowing in man the seed of total rebellion, that total rebellion of which he himself is the expression. Instead he succeeds in inducing man to turn towards the world, and to stray progressively in a direction opposed to the destiny to which he has been called. From that moment the world becomes the terrain of man's temptation: the terrain in which man turns his back on God in various ways and in varying degrees; a terrain of rebellion rather than of collaboration with the Creator; a terrain where human pride seeks not the glory of God but its own greater satisfaction. The world as a terrain for struggle between man and God, for the created being's defiance of his Creator. This is the great drama of history, myth and civilisation.

There is nothing of Prometheus in the biblical serpent. There is no vestige in Genesis of the context that would justify such an interpretation. All the same there has been, and still is, no lack of attempts to transplant the Prometheus myth into the soil of Genesis – attempts, that is, to prize man as if he were God. Here we have at its deepest level that age-long process of temptation of mankind, the history of denial. More superficially, however, it is recognisable in the unmistakeable and vigorous attraction exerted on mankind by the world.

During the last Synod of Bishops the German episcopate contributed a wide-ranging study of "Secularisation and secularism", a subject that cropped up again and again in the plenary discussions and in the individual language groups. Let one extract from the basic document suffice: "Secularisation, in the specific form it takes today, is a major obstacle in matters of religion. In the form of secularism, that is of a planned attack on religion and on belief in God, secularisation – especially when it is institutionalised in 'pseudo-ecclesial' forms – has become, by virtue of its claim to embrace the whole range of human behaviour, a sort of counter-religion".

It does seem however that it was Vatican II that made the essential distinction between secularisation and secularism, in article 36 of *Gaudium et spes* which explains the true meaning of the autonomy of earthly realities. It is worth pondering this text afresh, because it illustrates that interaction of Word and anti-Word which has its beginnings, as we have seen, in Genesis:

"Many of our contemporaries seem to fear that if human activity is too closely bound up with religion the autonomy of men, of society and of the sciences will be thwarted. If by the autonomy of earthly realities we mean that created things and even societies have laws and values proper to themselves, which mankind must gradually discover, use and regulate, then we are dealing with a legitimate demand which not only is put forward by men of our time but also is in conformity with the will of the Creator. ... Anyone who strives with humility and perseverance to fathom the secrets of reality is – without realising it – being as it were led by the hand of God who, in keeping all things in existence, makes them to be what they are. ... If, instead, the expression 'autonomy of earthly realities' is understood to mean that created things do not depend on God, and that man can handle them in such a way as not to relate them to the Creator, then no one who believes in God can fail to see how false such an interpretation is. Without the Creator the creature vanishes. Moreover, all believers, no matter what religion they profess, have always understood him to speak and make himself evident in the discourse of creatures. But forgetfulness of God leaves the creature itself devoid of understanding".

These words, which admirably contrast a correct understanding of the autonomy of earthly realities with an erroneous one, deserve careful thought. In the first covenant man was called upon to practise not only obedience towards God the Creator but also "justice". And even though fundamentally the term "justice" can be applied only to relationships between equals, we are not exaggerating when we think that man, who has made immense progress and has achieved the high level of culture and technical sophistication enjoyed by men today, now seems even more unjust towards God the Creator precisely because he is the man of progress. This is where the age-old drama of temptation of mankind is now being played out: between secularism and secularisation. While secularisation attributes to earthly things their due and rightful autonomy, secularism insists that the world must be taken away from God! And then? Then everything must be given to man! But can the world really be given to man more fully than it was given to him at the start of creation?

Can it be given to him in a different way? Can it be given independently of the objective order of being? of good? of evil? And supposing it were given in a different way, independently that is of the objective order, might it not rebound on man, reducing him to slavery? Might it not turn him into a mere tool? Nowadays one needs only to consider the progress made in nuclear physics alongside the attendant folly of armaments, the progress made in medicine alongside the attendant folly of contraception.[2] The conciliar text concerning the rightful autonomy of earthly realities and human institutions is applicable to all this: "... forgetfulness of God leaves the creature itself devoid of understanding" (*Gaudium et spes*, n. 36). What a wealth of meaning there is in those words!

Yet the anti-Word does not stop there. It goes further still and deeper still. What is said in the third chapter of Genesis seems to lead us all the way to the extreme form of denial, the one adopted by present-day man. The concept of alienation as formulated by Marx, or at least as formulated by his followers, has been applied – as we know – to religion. According to them religion has an alienating function. To alienate means, here, to de-humanise. By professing and practising a religion man deprives himself of his own right to his humanity and ascribes all prerogative to God, that is to say to a concept of his own devising – thus subordinating himself to one of his own products!

When the Devil says in the third chapter of Genesis: "your eyes would open and you would become like God", these words express the full range of temptation of mankind, from the intention to set man against God to the extreme form it takes today. We could even say that in the first stage of human history this temptation not only was not accepted but had not been fully formulated. But the time has now come: this aspect of the Devil's temptation has found the historical context that suits it. Perhaps we are experiencing the highest level of tension between the Word and the anti-Word in the whole of human history. Alienation thought of in that way implies not only denial of the God of the covenant but also of the very idea of God: denial of his existence and at the same time the postulate – and in a sense the imperative – of liberation from the very idea of God in order to bolster man.

Here is a typical extract from Feuerbach's book on religion: "In place of love of God we ought to acknowledge love of man as the only true religion; in place of belief in God we ought to expand man's belief in himself, in his own strength, the belief that humanity's destiny is dependent not on a being higher than humanity but on humanity itself, that man's only demon is man himself – primitive man, super-stitious, egoistic, evil – but that similarly man's only god is man himself".[3]

We may now be wondering if this is the last lap along that way of denial which started out from around the tree of the knowledge of good and evil. To us, who know the whole bible from Genesis to Revelation, no stretch of that route can come as a surprise. We accept with trepidation but also with trust the inspired words of the Apostle Paul: "Let no one deceive you in any way; because first it is necessary for the rebellion to come, and for the man of sin, the son of perdition, to reveal himself ..." (2 Thess 2,3).

Laicist anthropocentrism is even more opposed to admitting man's relationship with Satan than it is to acknowledging man's relationship with God or with any "sacrum". Man is alone, and his greatness requires that this be so: that he be alone, independent of good and evil, independent of God and of Satan. All the same, might not the perfection *sui generis* of temptation of man lie in precisely this, that man should believe himself to be alone? These are the perspectives of the third chapter of Genesis, which are now becoming more understandable – not so much in their original expression as in the light of the signs of our times.

Notes

1. "Our Father, deliver us from evil" (15.11. 1972).
2. Cf Karol Wojtyla, *Fruitful and responsible love.* St Paul Publications 1978.
3. Cf L. Feuerbach, *The essence of religion.*

V.

Meditation on the Joyful Mysteries

1. *The first mystery: the Annunciation*

We are about to go back to the source of the words we repeat every day as we pray the Holy Rosary. The angel Gabriel spoke those words to the Virgin of Nazareth: hence the author of each and every word is God himself, and each of them contains the reality it expresses. When the angel salutes Mary with the words: "Hail, full of grace!" (Lk 1,28), his greeting is fully congruous with the abundance of favour bestowed on the Blessed Virgin from the moment of her Immaculate Conception. The later words: "The Lord is with you! Blessed are you among women" refer to the same thing. The mystery of this choice, in which God remains free and at the same time leaves the human being free, leaves us full of amazement. In one sense – a very real sense – he waits to be chosen himself. Because freedom is an essential prerequisite for loving God and giving oneself to God.

The Virgin replies in a manner fully in harmony with her inner truth. Mary's inner truth was this: she had already made an unconditional choice and bestowed herself completely on her one and only divine spouse. That is why she was able to say: "How can this come about, since I know no man?" (Lk 1,34), and she said it immediately she heard the angel announce that she would conceive and give birth to the Son. For motherhood entails "knowing a man", and this is in direct contrast with her choice. When Mary asks her question she is not contesting the divine plan: she is simply remarking that motherhood "according to the flesh" is difficult to reconcile with the choice she had made "according to the Spirit".

Then the angel explains: "The Holy Spirit will come upon you, and the power of the most high will cover you with its shadow" (Lk 1,35). Mary still does not know how this will come about, but she does know one thing very clearly: that everything is bound to be consistent with her own choice made at the right moment according to the Spirit. So she says: "Behold the handmaid of the Lord; may it come about according to your word" (Lk 1,38). We may note that before expressing her "fiat" the Virgin bears witness to the Spirit who fills her whole soul, and to the Son she is to conceive and give birth to, when she says: "Behold the handmaid of the Lord!". We have reached the point in time when the new age begins. To this beginning, to the Annunciation, we must always return, because thanks to it the new age endures throughout human history, and with it the new man.

2. *The second mystery: the Visitation*

In Poland Our Lady's Visitation is lived in a way very special to us Poles. For nearly twenty years now we have had the pilgrimage of the portrait of the Black Madonna – or rather the faithful copy of it which was blessed by Pius XII in 1957 at the request of the Primate, Cardinal Wyszynski, in the name of the Polish episcopate. So in 1957 the pilgrimage began, and it goes on to this day and will continue to go on: from one diocese to the next, from one parish to the next, sometimes from one church to the next in the same parish. Thanks to an initiative on the part of both pastors and faithful, it is also customary for other paintings of the Black Madonna to be carried in *peregrinatio* from one house to another, from one family home to another. All this is possible thanks to deep religious experience, long and thorough spiritual preparation, willingness to undertake all-night vigils, and prayer that unites all parishioners, neighbours and members of families.

In these ways we try to re-live the first Visitation, that of Mary to her kinswoman Elizabeth at Ain-Karim. The words with which Elizabeth greeted the Virgin are well-known: "Blessed are you among women, and blessed is the fruit of your womb" (Lk 1,42). And then: "And why is it granted to me that the mother of my Lord should visit me? ... Blessed is she who believed that everything said to her at the Lord's behest would come true" (Lk 1,43–45). We take Mary into each parish, into each community of the People of God, as the one who was the first of all believers, the one who guides the People of God on its pilgrimage of faith, in the words of the second Vatican Council.

And when, after the first chapter of St Luke's gospel has been read, everybody joins in singing the Magnificat, one has the impression that Our Lady herself has put her own words into the mouths of our people. And a deep longing, too, is implicit: a longing for Mary to grant us the faith with which she, the Mother of God, sang her Magnificat; a longing to share in a special way in Mary's faith, the faith which can make us strong and resolute as we too maintain our stand close to Christ. "Blessed is she who believed. ..." (Lk 1,45).

3. *The third mystery: the Birth*

"God is born and the powers tremble – the Lord of the heavens lies naked. The star fades and the brilliance turns to shadow – the Infinite accepts limitation. Despised – re-clothed in glory, the mortal – the King of eternity".

That extract from a Polish Christmas carol is, in my opinion, outstandingly expressive of the mystery of God incarnate. It is a mystery embracing contrasts: light and the darkness of night, God's infiniteness and man's limitations, glory and humiliation, immortality and mortality, divinity and human poverty. People who are brought face to face with the "mysterium fascinosum"[1] of this holy Christmas night which makes all races one become conscious that what then happened was something immensely important, something without parallel in the history of mankind. The Nativity brings us within touching distance, so to speak, of our spiritual birth in God through grace.

Born through faith and grace, we have been called children of God; and so we are, says St John (cf 1 Jn 3,1).

This is the night of man's greatest exaltation: in what then happened man finds his own origin. The Son of God is born as a man by the power of the Holy Spirit, and the children of men become the adopted children of God, and so acquire the right to call God "Abba – Father" (Rom 8,15; Gal 4,6). The face of the earth is transformed in its essential dimension, and this interior transformation is owed directly to the Nativity; this is the principal reason for our Christmas rejoicing, for the joy we all feel: the magi and the shepherds, bishops, priests, children. "Genuit puerpera Regem" (Liturgy of the hours, Ant. 2): "She wrapped him in swaddling clothes and laid him in a manger, because there was no room for them at the inn" (Lk 2,7). Above this manger the angels sang their Gloria; to this manger came the shepherds and the royal magi. The manger was the place where God and mankind first met through faith. That meeting gave birth to the Church; and it gave birth to the hope of mankind, the hope that is continually born anew.

4. *The fourth mystery: the Presentation of Jesus in the temple*

Forty days after the Nativity the Church celebrates an event full of spiritual significance. On that day the Son of God, as a tiny child of poor parents, born in a rough out-house in Bethlehem, was carried to the temple in Jerusalem. This was his own temple, the temple of the living God; but he came to it not as the Lord but as one under the Law. For the poor the law prescribed that forty days after the birth of the firstborn two turtle-doves or two young pigeons must be offered in sacrifice, as a sign that the child was consecrated to the Lord (cf Lk 2, 22–24; Ex 13, 2.15; Lev 5,7; 12,8).

The message which the Spirit of God allowed the old man

Simeon to sense and express so wonderfully was implicit in the event itself, in this first encounter between the Messiah and his temple. On seeing the child, Simeon begins to utter words that are not of human provenance. He prophesies, prompted by the Holy Spirit; he speaks with the voice of God, the God for whom the temple was built and who is its rightful master.

We chose Simeon's words as the connecting thread in this retreat. They begin, in what the liturgy calls the Song, by bearing witness to the light, and in so doing they ante-date by thirty years the witness borne by John the Baptist. They end, on the other hand, by bearing the first witness to the cross, in which contradiction of Jesus, the Christ, is to find tangible expression.

The cost of the cross was shared by the mother, whose soul – according to Simeon's words – was to be pierced by a sword, "so that the thoughts of many hearts may be laid bare" (Lk 2,35).

Chronologically the Presentation of Jesus in the temple is linked with the Nativity, but in its significance it belongs with the mystery of the Pasch. It is the first of the events which clearly reveal the messianic status of the new-born child. With him are linked the fall and the rising of many in the old Israel and also the new. On him the future of mankind depends. It is he who is the true Lord of the ages to come (Is 9,6). His reign begins when the temple sacrifice is offered in accordance with the Law, and it attains full realisation through the sacrifice on the cross, offered in accordance with an eternal plan of love.

5. *The fifth mystery: Jesus among the doctors of the Law*

The episode of Jesus among the doctors is recounted by Luke with a surprising richness of detail. As in the account of the Presentation in the temple, so too in this we can discern the major theme of the mystery of the Incarnation, in which there is a dark veining of sadness as well as the radiance of joy. The source of the joy is grace, that of the sadness sin. The joy points to Emmanuel (Is 7,14; Mt 1,23), God present among his people; the sadness to the prospect of the cross, present in the inmost heart of Emmanuel and the hearts of those closest to him.

The mystery we are now considering has two dimensions, both of which must always be borne in mind.

There is the historical dimension of the event itself, which took place when Jesus was twelve years old. In accordance with ancient Jewish custom the entire holy family went to Jerusalem for the Passover, the greatest of Jewish feasts because it recalled the liberation from slavery in Egypt and the miraculous passage through the Red Sea. At the same time this celebration proclaimed the eventual coming of the messianic era and the messianic passing from servitude to freedom. This no doubt was the subject most discussed and pondered in the crowded temple on that occasion. So no wonder Jesus was found sitting among the doctors, listening and asking them questions; and no wonder either that "all who listened to him were amazed by his understanding and his answers" (Lk 2,46–47).

So much for the first aspect: the event, which includes the facts that Jesus stayed behind in the temple, was searched for by Mary and Joseph and was found after three days.

But, as we have pointed out, there is a second dimension: the event *of itself* provides clear expression of Jesus's messianic awareness. We do not know what he said to the doctors in the temple. But we do know that he answered his mother's anxious question with a gentle reproach: "Why did you go searching for me? Did you not know that I must attend to what concerns my Father? (Lk 2,49). And after those words Jesus withdrew into the silence of the home in Nazareth until he was thirty. "And his mother remembered these things in her heart" (Lk 2,51); that is what the Church does too, as she wends her way through the centuries.

Note

1. R. Otto, *The idea of the holy.*

VI.

The God who "cannot deny his own self"

1. *The Gospel truth*

"The world which (the Council) has in mind is the world of men, or rather the entire human family within the context of all the realities in the midst of which that family lives; the world which is the theatre of human history and which bears the marks of man's exertions, of his defeats and his victories, the world which Christians believe created and sustained by the Creator's love, a world undoubtedly once in bondage to sin but freed by the crucified and risen Christ and, with the Devil routed, destined for self-transformation and self-fulfilment, in accordance with the divine plan" (*Gaudium et spes*, n. 2).

How sorely we needed such a definition of the world! Not only so as to shape the text of the Pastoral Constitution itself but also so as to provide the key to understanding the signs of the times, and at the same time the key to the Church's own self-understanding – as expressed by the Council after careful analysis of all those signs which are classed as "contemporary", "of our own time". The Church in the world of today. Yet we also need to consider the *Kairos* of revelation (2 Cor 6,2; Gal 6,9–10; 2 Tim 4,2), the eschatological time of salvation, of fulfilment of the eternal divine plan. In which direction is the river of that time flowing, in the stormy conditions of today's world?

During the recent world congress of laity, in Rome in autumn 1975, there was considerable talk about God's silence, which some considered to characterise our times and produce a particularly trying climate. But at this point we ought to ask ourselves whether one really can talk along such lines. "Multifariam multisque modis olim Deus loquens patribus in prophetis, novissime diebus istis locutus est nobis in Filio" (Heb 1,1–2). God said everything when he spoke in the Son, who is his eternal Word. The only question is: whether the potential of the Word heard – *rationabile obsequium fidei* according to the standards of our time – is commensurate with the plenipotential of the Word spoken according to the standards of all time.

Let us try to go back once again to the beginning of this Word spoken by God. The third chapter of Genesis, in which Satan first appeared on the world horizon bringing sin, also includes the first proclamation of the coming of the Saviour, the Word incarnate, the Son. The proclamation of the incarnation of the Word, the eternally begotten Son of the Father, is a divine riposte to the first appearance in world history of the man of the anti-Word and the man of sin (cf 2 Thess 2,3).

"Then the Lord God said to the serpent: Because you have done this, be accursed among all the animals and all the wild beasts" (Gen 3,14).

The curse is God's riposte. It first appears here, in Genesis. It has the look of a seal placed by God on evil. From that moment it is clear that the universe, of which the visible structure brought revelation of nothing but good ("And God saw that this was good ... and God blessed them ...": the divine blessing is simply a seal placed on revelation of good) – it is clear that this world, in its deeper spiritual structure, is marred by a cleft between good and evil, blessing and curse.

Thus the conflict between good and evil entered the empirical world, and it entered men's hearts as well.

When God says: "I will put enmity ..." (Gen 3,15), these words are in no way a denial of the great heart so evident in the first chapters of Genesis. They quite simply affirm that this heart – and this heart only – is far above the conflict between good and evil; that this heart is far superior to all that, and therefore is the ultimate source of good. The God who is totally on the side of good and totally against evil does not cease to be a God of the covenant. Quite the reverse! God is far greater than this cleft in the world, this conflict brought about by one of his creatures. He is a greater God than ever, greater not only as the God of infinite majesty but also as the God of the covenant. He is a God who "cannot deny his own self" (2 Tim 2,13).

The divine Fatherhood is implicit in this revelation. The Father too, like the mother, sees with the heart, but perhaps in a more penetrating and more fundamental way. The Father's "raisons du coeur" – of which Pascal spoke – are different from those of the mother. Can we perhaps hear the beat of this fatherly heart all through that dramatic dialogue in the third chapter of Genesis? "The Lord God called Adam and said to him: Where are you? And he answered: I heard the sound of you in the garden and I was afraid because I was naked, and so I hid myself. And the Lord then said: Who showed you that you were naked? Did you perhaps eat the fruit of the tree which I forbade you to eat? Adam replied: It was the woman you gave me as my companion who gave me fruit from the tree, and I ate it. The Lord God said to the woman: Why did you do this? And the woman replied: The serpent led me astray and I ate the fruit" (Gen 3,9–13). Possessing consummate knowledge of good and evil, the Father sets in motion the process of reconstruction, of reparation. It is in this context that the words: "I will put enmity ..." take on their true meaning. The worst situations of all are the ones in which all distinction between good and evil is thrown to the winds: chaos then reigns.

That is why God says: "I will put enmity between you and the woman, between your seed and her seed: he will crush your head and you will trap him by the heel" (Gen 3,15). (The Vulgate uses a feminine pronoun in the second part of the sentence: "She will crush your head ...".) Here are the first rays of light to appear above the abyss, above the conflict between good and evil; it is the light of the Good

News of salvation. Tradition and theology have both called this passage the *proto-evangelium* because it includes the first proclamation of the Messiah, born of woman, who will deal Satan his mortal blow. The God of infinite majesty, the God of transcendence and absolute holiness, takes the good into his care and through salvation history prepares the way for its victory. Thus God declares himself to be the God of the covenant, which time and again he offers to man; the covenant which took final shape when he "novissime locutus est nobis in Filio" (Heb 1,2). Thus he reveals himself to be God of the covenant, the God who is always "the One who is greater"! Victorious over the baleful hatred of Satan, magnanimous towards natural human frailty. Always greater because he is Love. And so even the words of the curse reveal the God who is Truth and Love.

"The time is coming – said Jesus to the Samaritan woman – indeed it has now come, when true worshippers will worship the Father in spirit and in truth, because the Father wants worshippers of that kind. God is spirit, and those who worship him must worship him in spirit and in truth" (Jn 4,22–23).

From the moment of the very first denial, Truth – the divine Truth – will always seek, in ways known only to itself, to penetrate world history, to enter the minds and hearts of men. The father of lies will never cease to deny it. But the one who said of himself: "I am the way and the truth ..." (Jn 14,6) is certain of victory. The great heart that opened in the first chapters of Genesis does not withdraw and close again when faced with the lie, but sheds over the whole of human history, in every age including our own, the light of boundless hope.

2. *The economy of the Incarnation*

Let us now leave aside those pages of Genesis, so full of truth about man and the world, and try to look at this mystery of God from another angle. Who is this God, always greater

than the world, the world which "fell into slavery to sin"?
Who is this God of human history who is greater even than
time and space?

In Advent we recite in the liturgy of the hours those great
antiphons that are so wonderfully expressive of the noblest
hopes of the People of God, hopes that are all pinned on the
person of the One whose coming we await. Each day we give
him a different name:

> O Sapientia, quae ex ore Altissimi prodiisti
> O Adonai et dux domus Israel
> O radix Jesse
> O clavis David et sceptrum domus Israel
> O Oriens, splendor lucis aeternae
> O Rex gentium
> O Emmanuel rex et legifer noster.

But when he does arrive, the antiphons cease and all is
silence. And the human mind too is silenced: all its pro-
jections, all its reckonings fade into nothingness; one certainty alone remains: "God is totally Other". This is the
strongest possible proof that the one who has come is divine,
begotten of the Father. In him there is nothing of the great
leader, nor of the king, even though from the very beginning
he will be hounded and persecuted as a pretender to the
throne of Israel. He is defenceless – as are his mother and
the carpenter to whom the Father entrusted the earthly care
of his Son. He is defenceless and also, that Christmas night,
homeless; and then, almost immediately, an exile. Throughout
his life he shared the lot of the poorest in Israel, and for
thirty years remained in the shadows, in the silence of
Nazareth, with no means of gaining power or earthly
dominion. "Vere tu es Deus absconditus – Salvator"
(Is 45,15).

Christ's entry into the world reveals an economy altogether *sui generis*, proper to God alone. It is a divine
economy, with its source in the Father, the Son and the Holy
Spirit. From this source gush the waters of the great river

that extends over the entire surface of the earth and permeates the whole of history. "Out of the heart of him who believes in me – as scripture says – shall flow rivers of living water" (Jn 7,38). This living water runs through the life of every man and, regardless of all his purely temporal reckonings and criteria, flows through his heart and his actions without his being aware of it. Nowadays there are so many attempts to reduce everything in human life to statistics, to mathematical formulae. In some places, under some political systems, man himself seems lost in a forest of figures which are used as tools to regulate his existence. And man cannot remain oblivious of the great threat posed by this gigantic machine at the disposal of material power, or rather the many powers, the veritable imperialisms which vie endlessly with one another but which cannot ultimately claim to have at heart the good or the real happiness of mankind. Indeed the reverse is true: for those powers, those imperialisms, see in man – in man's freedom and inner truth – the biggest of all threats to themselves. The coming of Jesus of Nazareth into the world, the incarnation of the Word, is the revelation of a completely different economy. He who was sent by the Father (cf Lk 4,18; Jn 10,36) appears before our eyes as a thoroughly poor man all his life. "Foxes have their lairs and the birds of the air their nests; but the Son of man has nowhere to lay his head" (Mt 8,20). The quantifier in the divine economy – if one may speak in such terms – is totally different from the one used by the world. That is because God himself is totally Other. God wills himself "poor", he wills himself "defenceless" and "weak". The power that never deserted Jesus as he went about his teaching has nothing in common with the motives characteristic of human reasoning. Present-day political economy has fully mastered the techniques of buttressing the power of this world. By contrast Christ could say in all truth – not just once before Pilate but again before every power or political system in existence today – "My kingdom is not of this world" (Jn 18,36).

The world sorely needed a criterion of power that would be radically "other", a manifestation of a different hierarchy of values, in order that the men of those days and the men of today – even the most critical and suspicious of them – might come to believe in the truth of love. It is difficult to believe in love. "I don't believe in love", disillusioned youngsters will sometimes say. To say "I don't believe in love" is also the natural reaction of every man who is oppressed by evil or – worse still – caught in the toils of consumerism and a prey to the hunger for status symbols that divides both the world and the hearts of men. Jesus the Christ had to enter the world in the way he did, had to pass through and out of it in the way he did, in order that the whole of his passing – *phase, transitus Domini* – from start to finish might confirm the truth of love: "God loved the world so much that he sacrificed his only Son" (Jn 3,16).

Love goes hand-in-hand with poverty, its power none other than the utter weakness of the incarnate Word in the stable at Bethlehem and on the cross. He sought nothing except the good of those who were his own. An Anglican theologian, John Robinson, has called him "the man for others". He sought nothing but the good of mankind, "so that all who believe in him may not perish but may have everlasting life" (Jn 3,16). Love is a force, the driving force in salvation. Man – even the man who is far distant from the Gospel – is capable of recognising the close tie between love and salvation. The concentration camps will always remain in men's minds as real-life symbols of hell-upon-earth; they expressed to the highest degree the evil that man is capable of inflicting on his fellowmen. In one such camp Fr Maximilian Kolbe died in 1941. All the prisoners knew that he died of his own free choice, offering his own life in exchange for that of a fellow-prisoner. And with that particular revelation there passed through that hell-upon-earth a breath of fearless and indestructible goodness, a kind of intimation of salvation. One man died, but humanity was saved! So close is the tie between love and salvation. In this way love became the foundation for Christ's victory, the victory proclaimed in advance by God in the third chapter of Genesis: "He will crush your head ...". Christ is the one who was proclaimed in advance, the one who fulfils the promise; thus the *proto-evangelium* and the Gospel merge.

In seeking the good of mankind and of all creation, he gives the Father the glory that is his due. This is another element, an essential criterion, in the divine economy. "The glory of God is man alive", St Irenaeus once said. This dimension is totally unknown to the economy of the world. Man is "a being on the way to death", asserts one German existentialist. Man is "a being on the way to glory", declares the one who was born in a stable and died on the cross like a slave (cf Jn 17,22).

Precisely for all these reasons God is always "the one who is greater". "Because if our own hearts condemn us, God is greater ..." (1 Jn 3,20), and it is he who from the very beginning is present in the history of the human heart. And "if we deny him, he will deny us", but even "if we are not faithful, he remains faithful, because he cannot deny his own self" (2 Tim 2,12–13).

VII

He who is Gift and the source of all giving

1. *Word and Love*

Let us turn our thoughts to God who is gift and the source of all giving.

The fathers of the second Vatican Council were convinced that the complex reality of the Church cannot be adequately expressed in societal terms alone, even when the society constituted by the Church is called the "People of God". In order properly to describe this reality and appreciate its underlying significance it is necessary to return to the dimension of mystery, that is to the dimension of the most Holy Trinity. That is why the Constitution *Lumen gentium* starts with an introductory account of the divine economy of salvation, which ultimately is a trinitarian economy (cf *Lumen gentium*, nn.2–4):

"Adhering to a mysterious plan all his own, one of wisdom and goodness, the eternal Father created the universe, decided to endow men with a share in his own divine life and did not abandon them when in Adam they fell but always sent them aids to salvation, having in mind Christ the redeemer 'who is the image of the invisible God, born before any creature' (Col 1,15)" (n.2).

"Therefore the Son came, sent by the Father who, before the foundation of the world, in him chose us and predestined us to be adopted as sons, for in him the Father wished to gather all things together (cf Eph 1,4.5.10)" (n.3).

"Once the work on earth entrusted to the Son by the Father had been accomplished, on the day of Pentecost the Holy Spirit was sent, in order constantly to sanctify the

Church and enable believers to have access to the Father through Christ in the one Spirit (cf Eph 2,18)" (n.4).

If our thoughts were to take their cue from the Council document they might now proceed from the point in history when the Church was founded. Yet the history of salvation goes right back to the history of the creation of man. We know very well that the "mysterious plan" of which *Lumen gentium* speaks, the plan of salvation, was worked out in the Son, who is the fully appropriate Word. St John fixes our attention on the Word when he writes: "In him (the Word) was the life, and the life was the light of men. And the light shone in the darkness; but the darkness did not overpower it" (Jn 1,3–5). So the darkness of the anti-Word did not destroy the divine plan of truth and life, God's project in the third chapter of Genesis, the consequences of which affect generation after generation. But together with the anti-Word there appeared in the spiritual history of the world an anti-Love, referred to by St Augustine as "amor sui usque ad contemptum Dei".[1] This anti-Love dealt a severe blow to the original covenant which, together with the work of creation, was offered to men by the great heart.

We already found traces of that great heart in our earlier meditations, but we must now try to go more deeply still into the mystery of the Love which, with the Word, is co-existent with the Father and is eternal. This mystery is part of the deeper mystery of God's personal being, that of the most Holy Trinity. And although this Love – as gift from the Father to the Son and from the Son to the Father, uncreated gift – makes its appearance later in revelation, it must somehow have been present in the economy which gave rise to creation, salvation and the covenant.

Are we right in saying "later"? In the very first lines of Genesis we read: "In the beginning God created heaven and earth. The earth was a formless void: darkness shrouded the abyss and over the waters hovered the Spirit of God. God said: 'Let there be light', and light there was. God saw that light was good" (Gen 1,1–4). When we re-read this declaration, with its praise of the good implicit in the created world, it is impossible not to perceive Love, even though we still lack evidence strong enough to allow us to think of that Love as a distinct person. I mean that in the isolated context of Genesis alone we cannot interpret the sentence "Over the waters hovered the Spirit of God" in the sense of the Holy Spirit who came down upon the Apostles on the day of Pentecost (cf Acts 2,1–13). All the same, the wider context of the bible as a whole could, I think, suggest an interpretation of that kind, allowing us to understand the earlier texts in the light of the later ones. Thus we can perceive in the Spirit of God which "hovered over the waters" the eternal person who is Love, who together with the Word was present at the start of creation and the inauguration of the covenant.

Love, an uncreated gift, is part of the inner mystery of God and is the very nucleus of theology. In creation and in the covenant Love is made manifest not only as motive but also as fact, as reality, a consequence of divine working. Precisely for this reason, the world that emerged from the hands of God the Creator is itself structured on a basis of love. To be something created is to be something "endowed", above all with existence and, together with existence, nature – which reflects different levels of being, differing degrees of perfection and good in the world, from inferior beings to more perfect ones, although St Thomas declares that every being is perfect according to its kind.

This is proved in a very special way in the case of man. Can we not discern from the second chapter of Genesis that not only was the world around Adam and Eve a gift to them but also that they themselves were, each of them, a gift bestowed on the other, and that reciprocity was to be the mark of their lives as human beings of differing sexes? "And Adam and his wife were both naked, and they were not ashamed of this" (Gen 2,25). Love, which itself is gift, uncreated gift, ineffable, communicating itself to men as grace, gives one the impression that one is receiving the gift

of the world, but especially the gift of one's humanity, the
man's masculinity, the woman's femininity, the procreative
ability of both. Isn't that, to this day, the truth about love
which married couples in their hearts believe in? Sin, which
is what the third chapter of Genesis is all about, destroys this
sense of being "endowed" with the world and with, above all,
each other. "Then the eyes of both opened and they saw that
they were naked" (Gen 3,7). In place of deep awareness of
the gift of creation, of the gift of another human being, in
place of love there appears that threefold concupiscence
which St John said could never come from the Father
(1 Jn 2,16). Careful study of human origins – which seems
particularly important today if we are to understand the
crucial problems of anthropology and ethics – enables us to
discover, together with the mystery of the Father and the
Word, the third mystery of God's personal unity: the Love,
uncreated gift, lying at the root of all created gifts.

In the liturgy of Pentecost[2] we sing: "Spiritus Domini
replevit orbem terrarum: et hoc, quod continet omnia
scientiam habet vocis". It is he who speaks through the
testimony of every creature, for it is he who has given them a
voice with which to speak. It is he, the Holy Spirit, who
spoke by means of the prophets through the history of the
people of the covenant ("qui locutus est per prophetas":
Credo). It is he, finally, whose action enabled the eternal
Word, of one being with the Father and himself, to be made
flesh.

2. *The Son and the Holy Spirit*

"How can this come about, since I know no man?", asks the
holy Virgin at Nazareth. "The Holy Spirit will come upon
you; and the power of the most high will cover you with its
shadow: therefore the holy child who will be born will be
called the son of God" (Lk 1,34–35).

"Holy" ... The son of God, as man, is a work of the
Spirit, a work of that same love, that same gift whose

presence and activity we perceived in our examination of the
first chapters of Genesis. But here this activity is given direct
expression and called by its proper name. The one who was
conceived by the Virgin in the Holy Spirit and was born one
night at Bethlehem is an eternal Son, whom the Father
"consecrated and sent into the world" (Jn 10,36). At the
same time he is a more perfect manifestation of gift, that
uncreated gift which is the Spirit of love who alighted on the
world to fulfil one mission at the moment of the Incarnation
and then, once the work of redemption had been accomplished, was again sent at the time of the Church's birth, as
the second Vatican Council reminds us in the Constitution
Lumen gentium.

Jesus the Christ is a man endowed with the Holy Spirit in
a way wholly unique. It is from him that we have continually
received "grace upon grace" (Jn 1,16).

When Jesus went to the bank of the Jordan, John the
Baptist exclaimed: "He will baptise you with the Holy Spirit
and with fire" (Mt 3,11; Jn 1,33). When he spoke for the
first time in the synagogue in Nazareth, he took his text
from the words of the prophet Isaiah: "The Spirit of the
Lord is upon me" (Lk 4,18; Is 61,1). In his nocturnal
conversation with Nicodemus he forcefully declared that "...
anyone who is not re-born through water and the Holy Spirit
cannot enter the kingdom of God" (Jn 3,5). Finally when,
after his resurrection, he came into the upper room through
closed doors, he related his first Easter words, and his own
mission, to the Holy Spirit: "Receive the Holy Spirit" (cf
Jn 20,22).

Jesus, the Christ formed by the Holy Spirit, brings with
him that same Spirit, imparts him to others and upon him
builds the universality of the kingdom of God on earth. If we
were to pursue the line of thought suggested by those highly
important words, we would arrive at the conclusion that
Jesus built his Church not so much upon himself as upon the
Holy Spirit. He, Jesus the Christ, is only a servant (cf
Mk 10,45) – the servant of Yahweh in the Old Testament

(Is 42,1) – a servant of the covenant (cf 2 Cor 3,6) who will fulfil his destiny in dependence on the Spirit who is gift! That new and definitive covenant will restore for ever to the world and to mankind the sense of receiving as gift everything there is: every created being, every material good, all the treasures of heart and mind; and first and foremost the sense of receiving as gift one's humanity, one's dignity as a human person and – something incomparably superior – one's dignity as an adopted child of God himself (cf 1 Jn 3,2). "Unless you become like little children, you will not enter the kingdom of heaven" (Mt 18,3). This "gift from on high", the Holy Spirit, restored to mankind – to human relationships, to marriage, to the family, to the various social groupings, to nations and to states – the fundamental sense of gift and of being "bestowed". This kind of awareness is a fruit of the Spirit of Christ; it results from irradiation by love, which puts a fundamentally different complexion on all these relationships and systems. From this awareness there ought to flow a different culture and a different civilisation, different relationships in the production and distribution of material goods, a different understanding of value and super-value. "The Spirit of the Lord is upon me" (Lk 4,18).

It thus becomes clear that the Council expressed the truth about the Church not only in the Dogmatic Constitution *Lumen gentium* but also in the Pastoral Constitution, *The Church in the world of today*: the truth about the Church present in every sphere of life and in all human activities – marriage, the family, the cultural, economic and political worlds and the international scene – as guardian and protector of justice and peace. In all these fields we must always rediscover the law of gift. With this principle as basis it will be possible, patiently but also effectively, to overcome all that has engendered and still does engender the anti-Love which St Augustine expressed so incisively in the formula: "amor sui usque ad contemptum Dei". This "amor sui usque ad contemptum Dei" in its various forms and dimensions lies at the root of all the ruthless exploitation of men by other men: exploitation in industrial production and consumerism, exploitation by the state in the various totalitarian or crypto-totalitarian systems which start off by issuing strongly humanistic declarations but end up by violating the most elementary of human rights. Finally, it is again the "amor sui usque ad contemptum Dei" that divides society into warring classes, that puts armaments in the hands of entire nations to enable them to fight one another and even engage in civil wars, and that divides the earth into so-called "worlds" which know only how to do battle with one another. ...

3. *"Amor Dei usque ad contemptum sui"*

"Amor sui usque ad contemptum Dei": that anti-Love which entered the history of man and of creation, can be countered and overcome – as St Augustine teaches us – only by love, boundless love, that is to say "Amor Dei usque ad contemptum sui"! The Holy Spirit prepared the servant of Yahweh for this act of love when through the mouth of Isaiah he predicted his Passion:

"Our ills he bore, our sufferings he endured; but we regarded him as one smitten, struck down by God and humiliated. But he was pierced for our betrayals, *struck down for our sins;* the punishment which would have restored health to us fell on him, and *in his wounds lies healing for us.* We all, like sheep, were going astray, each one going his own way, and *in him the Lord struck at the sins of us all ..."* (Is 53,4–6).

Jesus the Christ, who "wherever he went did good" (Acts 10,38), knew that through his departure from the world to return to the Father he was to prepare the way for the coming of the Holy Spirit. During his last talk with his Apostles, recounted in such detail by John, Jesus constantly turns their thoughts and their hearts in this direction: "If you love me, keep my commandments. And I will pray to the Father, who will give you another comforter to stay with you for ever, the Spirit of truth, whom the world cannot receive because it does not see him or know him; but you know him because he lives with you and will be in you. I will not leave you orphaned ..." (Jn 14,15–18).

"I have told you these things while I am still with you. But the comforter, the Holy Spirit, whom the Father will send in my name, will teach you all things and will remind you of all that I have said to you" (Jn 14,25–26).

Jesus predicts his second coming which, like the first, is to be prepared for by the Holy Spirit, this time not in the womb of the Virgin but in that of the whole Mystical Body. That is why, after the consecration in the Eucharist, the Church declares: "We proclaim your death, Lord, we proclaim your resurrection, as we await your coming". And immediately afterwards – in the third eucharistic prayer – the priest adds: "May he make us an everlasting sacrifice* pleasing to you". In Polish we say: a gift. This means: Lord, may that Love which is a gift embrace us and transform us – and with us, and by means of us, embrace and transform everything there is.

Jesus left us love as his commandment. Love was to be the main prop and stay of the spiritual identity of his followers as they faced the hatred which at various times and in various forms was to be hurled at them by the world. "If the world hates you, know that before hating you it hated me" (Jn 15,18).

The fact that the world hates is due to the existence of the anti-Love: "amor sui usque ad contemptum Dei". Jesus knows that this anti-Love will catch him up and, quoting Psalm 35, speaks of those who hate for no reason. Immediately, however, he returns to the perspective of the all-conquering love that he brought into the world, the "amor Dei usque ad contemptum sui".

"But when the comforter has come, whom I shall send you from the Father, the Spirit of truth who proceeds from the Father, he will bear witness to me; and you too will bear witness to me because you have been with me from the beginning" (Jn 15,26–27). And then Jesus explains why it is necessary for him to go to the Father: "But now I am going to him who sent me; yet none of you asks me: Where are you going? Instead, because I have told you these things sadness fills your hearts. But I am telling you the truth: it is better for you that I should go away; because if I do not go away the comforter will not come to you; but if I go away I will send him to you" (Jn 16,5–8).

Somebody once wrote that love is many-sided. How true! Love certainly has many dimensions. The love that Jesus speaks of in his farewell discourse has the dimension of the sacrifice which he himself is about to make, so it has an historical dimension that speaks to man with all the majesty of the cross. Yet at the same time love has a supra-historical dimension that goes beyond history, the dimension of a gift refused by the "amor sui usque ad contemptum Dei" of Satan, and very often distorted or destroyed in the hearts and the history of mankind. This gift must therefore return, by way of Jesus, to its source, so that man may rediscover himself within the covenant in all its fulness. That is the "why" of the cross. That is why Jesus leaves the upper room and begins the final stage of his journey towards the cross. God, who from the beginning wishes to be a gift to mankind and who is the overflowing source of all giving, is revealed in the mystery of the cross. "Deus absconditus" (Is 45,15).

Notes

1. St Augustine, *De civitate Dei*, XIV, 28.
2. Entrance antiphon, Pentecost (Wis 1,7).
* The talk being given in Italian, the speaker refers to the Italian translation. In English, we also use the word "gift". [Ed.]

VIII.

The price of redemption

1. *Jesus's hour*

Leaving that upper room in the highest part of Jerusalem, Jesus went down with his Apostles to the river Kedron (Jn 18,1). The descent was rapid, because that part of the city is built on a cliff with the river flowing at its foot. Jesus crossed the river and went with his followers into an olive-grove. By that time night had fallen, the night that preceded his fateful day, "his hour" (Jn 2,4; 7,30; 13,1). "What shall I say? Father, save me from this hour! But it is for this very purpose that I have come to this hour" (Jn 12,27).

We all know his Gethsemane hour, and we shall return to it again in another meditation. Let us simply recall that the Father did not take the cup away from his Son. The prayer of Gethsemane, in which a true man was expressing before God all the psychological and existential truth about fear in the face of suffering and death, ends with acceptance of the timeless decision whereby the Father "did not spare his own Son" (Rom 8,32) but made him "become sin for our sake" (2 Cor 5,21). This is a decision that neither the first man nor Satan could possibly have understood.

The words of the *proto-evangelium* said: "I shall place enmity between you and the woman, between your seed and her seed: he will crush your head and you will trap him by the heel" (Gen 3,15). These are words full of mystery: they disclose what is to come but the strictly divine meaning of it all remains hidden.

We should bear in mind that this true man who, humanly

speaking, is now left with his prayer to the Father unanswered, is the same man who at twelve years old had said:
"Why did you go searching for me? Did you not know that I
must attend to what concerns my Father" (Lk 2,49). He
spoke those words to his mother and Joseph after their three
days of troubled and anxious searching. The words of the
twelve-year-old now acquire their full value and meaning:
now, when he is on his knees in Gethsemane, when the
Father makes it clear to him that he must drink to the bitter
end the cup which his human nature shudders to contemplate. Jesus rises from prayer to return to those he thought
would keep vigil with him: to Peter, James and John who had
failed to fight off sleep. Then he says to them: "Sleep, then,
and rest: behold, the hour is near ... the one who is
betraying me is approaching" (Mt 26,45–46). At this
moment we glimpse again the twelve-year-old adolescent who
said to his mother with such conviction: "Why did you go
searching for me? ... I must attend to what concerns my
Father".

We are face to face with the inner truth of this man
foretold by the prophet Isaiah as the "servant of Yahweh",
the truth which shaped the whole of his inner life: "I always
do what is pleasing to him" (Jn 8,29).

When he expressed this for the first time, his mother
"remembered all these things in her heart", even though a
few lines earlier the evangelist says: "But they did not
understand what he was saying to them" (Lk 2,50).

Adolescents sometimes have secrets which they jealously
guard even from their parents. The twelve-year-old Jesus,
too, kept strictly to himself one great secret bound up with
his coming into the world: "Victims and offerings give you
no pleasure. ... Then I said: Behold, I come, that I may do
your will" (Ps 40(39),7–9). From the start Mary found
herself in the presence of this secret, the mystery of her son's
mission. And "she remembered all these things in her heart".
She had to remember. ... Every mother has to remember. ... Above all she had to remember, and live ever more

profoundly, his annunciation and conception. She conceived him as a true mother, he was her true son; but she conceived him also as "the handmaid of the Lord": "not of blood, nor of the will of the flesh, nor of the will of man, but of God" (Jn 1,13). And then she gave birth to him at night in a rough out-house, and soon afterwards had to flee to Egypt. But before that Simeon's words had rung in her ears: "Behold, he is a sign of contradiction ... for your part a sword will pierce your soul ..." (Lk 2,34). Mary could not fail to remember them.

We do not know if at that moment she recalled the words of Genesis: "I will place enmity ...". Be that as it may, it was that pronouncement that bound her destiny to his. And it even seems to place her, the woman, in the foreground: "I will place enmity between you and the woman", says God to Satan. Yet Mary was – in the words of a song much loved and often sung by young people in Poland – "quiet and beautiful as springtime; she lived in simplicity in all things, like us ...". She was quiet, saying little, living wholly absorbed in the mystery of her son. But "enmity" was nonetheless a fact: the "amor sui usque ad contemptum Dei" had to be finally routed in its struggle with the "amor Dei usque ad contemptum sui".[1] And the mother's heart could · not flee from the conflict for which her son was getting ready: "A sword will pierce your soul". This was her right as a mother – her privilege as a mother – the grace bestowed on her as the mother of the redeemer.

When the Gospel adds, after recording the words of the twelve-year-old Jesus: "But they did not understand what he was saying to them" (Lk 2,50), it means that even she, his mother, did not understand. Even so, one thing is certain: she was always willing to understand and accept everything to the full. "Behold the handmaid of the Lord ..." (Lk 1,38); as she spoke those words she conceived him in her womb.

2. *The all-important duty*

Humanly speaking, Mary could not have been surprised that
her son left home. It was something perfectly normal. Once
they reach a certain age children do leave their parents. They
go out into the world to take up their calling, as is commonly
said. So Jesus too left the family circle, once when he was
twelve and then, for good, when he was about thirty.

At the time when Jesus leaves to take up his public
ministry we find him with his mother – but already with
disciples as well – attending the wedding feast at Cana in
Galilee. St John has given us in his gospel a detailed
description of all that happened there (cf Jn 2,1–11). This
was the occasion of Jesus's first miracle, in which Mary had
a part to play. Let us recall it carefully. Let us remember the
words, heavy with meaning, exchanged by mother and son:
the mother's request: "They have no more wine" (Jn 2,3);
Jesus's reply: "Woman, what are you asking of me? My hour
has not yet come" (Jn 2,4). It is a highly significant reply.
Mary must have heard in it an echo of what she had earlier
heard from the lips of the twelve-year-old. It again faces her
with that hidden Father: "I always do what is pleasing to
him" (Jn 8,29). But this time the gospel-writer does not add:
"But they did not understand what he was saying to them".
Quite the reverse! Mary turns to the servants and says: "Do
whatever he tells you" (Jn 2,5). From this it is possible to
conclude that Mary knew what the Father willed. And that
she also knew, without any doubt, that her son would not
reject her request. Mary's request and the Father's will
coincided.

It is perfectly normal for children, whether adolescents or
adults, to leave home and set out in the direction of their own
choice of life. Obviously, then, the thirty-year-old son of
Mary setting off from home will go in the one and only
direction for which he came into the world. And it is also
perfectly normal and right for those children, even if they do
go away, to keep always in their hearts a great love for their

mothers. It is a love quite different from that of the young
child, although it is the same at bottom. As the personality
develops the love becomes more mature and at the same time
deeper. But if this love is to mature in the child's mind, it is
essential that the mother should not seek to hold him back
for herself but should follow him in spirit. Such mothers
respect the inner secrets of their children, who have been
brought up so to speak under their wings and who at a given
moment want to fly off relying on their own wing-power. The
great messianic wings of the will of the Father, on which the
son of Mary relies when he flies off from Nazareth, can be
discerned in the reply – at first sight a little puzzling – which
he gave when he was told: "Your mother and your brethren
are outside and would like to speak to you". His reply was:
"Who is my mother, and who are my brethren? ... whoever
does the will of my Father who is in heaven is my brother
and my sister and my mother" (Mt 12,48.50).

Those words, which express deep conviction of his
messianic mission of salvation, cannot be taken to indicate
lack of sensitivity or indifference towards his mother. Christ,
having embarked on this great mission – which already at
the age of twelve he regarded as his all-important duty –
certainly does not publicly question or in any way violate the
sacred rights of his mother. These rights are enshrined in the
Decalogue of the covenant with his people: "Honour your
father and your mother, as the Lord your God commands
you" (Deut 5,16). We know very well that those words are a
basic factor in the order of things that stems from the
Father: the Son came into the world precisely in order to
stress the importance of the covenant, to write it into men's
hearts. He came to seal it with his own blood, to pay "a high
price" (1 Cor 6,20; 7,23).

"Did you not know that I must attend to what concerns
my Father?" (Lk 2,50).

I must ... duty ... the all-important duty.... "This is the
whole meaning of my life and death". "What concerns my
Father". ... But what is it that concerns the Father? "It is

the good, the greater good of mankind, of myself and of my mother". It is the universal good, *bonum universi*[2], as St Thomas defined it. The good not only of this finite human world, of the earth which is "man's fatherland", as Saint-Exupéry[3] calls it, but the universal good: the order of being. This order and this good can be measured only by comparison with the timeless standards of God himself, the standards of wisdom and of love, of the Word and of the Spirit. Christ carries those standards within himself.

And in turn – simply because it was God who bestowed existence on the universe – the whole cosmos looks to Christ; it calls to Christ with the voice of all created things, as St Paul wrote in that wonderful passage in his letter to the Romans: "The whole creation waits with great longing for the children of God to be revealed ... in the hope that ... it will be freed from enslavement to decay so as to share in the freedom of the glory of the children of God" (8, 19–21). Thus speaks the Apostle of Jesus, divining the thought of his master thanks to some mysterious intuition. And thus Christ, the son of Mary, is thinking when he answers: "... whoever does the will of my Father who is in heaven is my brother and my sister and my mother" (Mt 12,50); thus speaks Jesus Christ: "He who is the Father has consecrated me and sent me out into the world" (Jn 10,36). And he duly went.

Now he is going away.... . At this moment he is rising to his feet in the garden of olives. Has he perhaps forgotten his mother's rights? It is to her that he owes his having become the Son of man, true man, true created being. It is to her that he is indebted for that.

His indebtedness to his mother is apparent in him every day of his life; it shows itself in his kindness of heart, in his human sensitivity to the beauties of nature. When little children are brought to him he blesses them, laying his hands on them (Mk 10,16); and when he rebukes the disciples, saying: "Let the little children come to me and do not stand in their way" (Mk 10,14; Lk 18,16), his mother too is, in a way, present in those words. And they are words in which he pays her tribute, for they recall his own childhood spent in the home she made at Nazareth where he thrived in the climate created by her love and motherly protection.

Jesus Christ was the living expression of his all-important duty – the duty he owed to the Father – which was deeply engraved in his whole being both human and divine; but he also respected the rights of his mother: "Honour your father and your mother". These two orders of duty owed were woven together in the depth of his personal being. They interacted when he ate in the company of publicans and sinners (cf Mk 2,16; Mt 9,11; Lk 5,30; 15,2); when he did not condemn the adulterous woman but simply said to her: "Go, and sin no more!" (Jn 8,3–11.)

In all that Jesus did and taught there was new and complete revelation of the great heart – the Father; but the heart thus revealed had all the profoundly human characteristics that he had inherited from his mother. This great heart, this Fatherhood of God, the Fatherhood already revealed in the pages of Genesis, was further revealed time and again in Jesus and through Jesus, his Son. That was the work the Father gave him to do (Jn 17,4). The Apostle Paul, in a great burst of spiritual exaltation, was to write of this work: "Blessed be the God and Father of our Lord Jesus Christ, who has blessed us with every spiritual blessing in Christ ... as he chose us in him even before the foundation of the world ... predestining us for adoption as his children through Jesus Christ ... in whom we have redemption through his blood, remission of sins, according to the richness of his grace which he (God) has lavished upon us" (Eph 1,3–8). And further on, no less emphatically: "For this reason I fall on my knees before the Father ... so that you may understand with all the saints the breadth, the length, the height and the depth (of this mystery) and know the love of Christ which surpasses all knowledge, so that you may be filled with all the fulness of God" (Eph 3,14–19).

3. *"Alma Socia Christi"*

That is how the Apostle Paul described the paschal mystery of Jesus Christ, the moment in time when mystery expressed itself in terms of historical fact, when it was marked once and for all with the sign of the cross on Mount Calvary and sealed by the last words of the crucified Christ: "Father, into your hands I commend my spirit" (Lk 23,46). That is how Paul described it. ... But from the very beginning Jesus was the living expression of that mystery of which St Paul speaks, and when he fell on his knees in Gethsemane he was like a living sacrifice (cf Rom 12,1), one condemned by God. The Father sacrificed, and "made to become sin for us", the very one who was a stranger to sin (cf 2 Cor 5,21), the one whom nobody could convict of sin (Jn 8,46). Is it really possible that he alone was deserted by the heart whose infinite love was revealed to men in the parable of the prodigal son and so many other parables?

When Jesus talked with the Father in the garden of olives, he had become conscious of the full extent of his all-important duty, the duty he had already spoken of to his mother when he was twelve. But one might also say that in this conversation with the Father it is possible to perceive an expression of his indebtedness to his mother, the duty he owed to her. For it is as a true son of man that Jesus talks with the Father. He expresses all the psychological truth of his human nature which shudders at the prospect of suffering and death. When he said: "If it is possible, let this cup pass from me" (Mt 26,39), he spoke – I think this can legitimately be said – in the name of his mother, to whom he owed his humanity together with that dread of suffering and death which is proper to human nature. He respected her rights to the very end: in Gethsemane and then on Mount Calvary. His suffering extended over the whole range of human sensitivity inherited from his mother, that same sensitivity that had made him appreciative of little children (cf Mk 9,36), the lilies of the field and the birds of the air (cf

Lk 12,24–27) and all the beauties of creation. He suffered therefore in all the mystery of his Person, in all the indescribable depth of his nature as God-man, the one and only subject and the one and only author of redemption of the world.

He respected his mother's rights to the very end: indeed he drew her into the ambit of the mystery of redemption, close to his own divine-human nature. When he said in Gethsemane: "Father, let this cup pass from me ..." he at once added: "if you are willing". And he ended by saying: "not my will but yours be done" (Lk 22,42). Yet in saying that he did not in any way overrule the rights the mother had to her son, to his life, to his good name. No, he most certainly did not overrule them! He knew that she, at the very start of the mystery, had made her decision: "Behold the handmaid of the Lord; may it come about according to your word ..." (Lk 1,38). All of it, to the very end!

Jesus Christ – true God and true man – knew he could rely on his mother as he pursued his mission within the framework of his all-important duty and thus carried out the will of the Father. He knew he could rely on his mother. ... He was sure of her heart, that heart which helped him to express in human fashion, in terms of human thoughts and feelings, the great heart of the Father. This motherly heart did not fail him at the testing time of Gethsemane and Calvary. It was close to him on the road from Pilate's praetorium to Mount Calvary as he carried his cross, and it was close to him when he drew his last breath. She was there; and with her were John the Apostle and Mary Magdalen (cf Jn 19,25–26). And even from the cross Jesus once again firmly asserted his mother's role in the mystery of redemption and of the Church, saying to John: "Behold your mother" and to the Mother, "Behold your son" (Jn 19,26–27). These words belong in his testament.

The mystery of salvation, that all-important duty entrusted by the Father to the Son, will be the subject-matter of several later meditations. One could even say that everything we shall be pondering during this retreat is directly concerned with that fundamental aspect of the mystery of salvation expressed in the words: "You have been redeemed at a high price ..." (1 Cor 7,23).

Man – quite obviously – could not save the world, just as he could not create it. These two great works – *magnalia Dei* – are on a par with one another. But God nevertheless wanted mankind to play a part in the redemption and salvation of the world: "He who created you without your help will not save you without your cooperation".[4] God assigned the principal creaturely role in this work of salvation to the Mother of Christ: *Alma Socia Christi.*[5]

Notes

1. St Augustine, *De civitate Dei*, xiv, 28.
2. St Thomas, *Quaestiones disputatae*, v,II, a.8, *De spiritualibus creaturis.*
3. A. Saint-Exupéry, *Vol de nuit*, Gallimard, Paris 1931.
4. St Augustine, *Sermo* 169,13.
5. Pius XII, Apostolic Constitution *Munificentissimus Deus.*

IX

Meditation on the Sorrowful Mysteries

---

1. *The first mystery: Jesus in Gethsemane*

None of the disciples was at all surprised that after the Last Supper Jesus crossed the river Kedron. It was night. And he often "pernoctabat in oratione" (Lk 6,12), spent the whole night in prayer.

Even the fact that he withdrew a short distance from them, taking with him only Peter, James and John, was nothing new. They had been with him on Mount Tabor too (Mk 9,2; Lk 9,28, etc).

The disciples were stretched to their limit after all that they had just experienced in the upper room. They could not forget the words spoken by the Master in the course of supper, words full of mystery: "This is my body offered in sacrifice for you; this is the cup of my blood, for the new and everlasting covenant, poured out for you ..." (cf Mt 26, 26–28, etc). The calm solemnity of that Passover meal had been disturbed by a strong current of anxiety and apprehensiveness. The Master had in fact said quite openly: "One of you is going to betray me" (Jn 13,21). And at that moment Judas, the one who had charge of the money, went out (cf Jn 13, 29–30). What is more, Jesus had said to Peter: "You, this very night, before the cock has crowed three times you will deny me three times" (Mk 14,30). Yet Peter had declared himself willing to die with him when the Master had said: "Satan insists on having you all, so as to sift you all like wheat. But I have prayed for you, Simon, that your faith may not fail; and you, once you are a changed man, you are to lend strength to your brethren" (Lk 22,31–32).

Gethsemane: a place of intense loneliness for Jesus, of almost total dereliction as he faced his Passion. It was a kind of bloodless foretaste of the Passion, although the gospel-writer does tell us that his sweat fell to the ground like drops of blood (cf Lk 22,44). The inner reality of Jesus's agony in Gethsemane remained hidden from his disciples, who in any case had fallen asleep from emotional exhaustion (cf Lk 22,45). His suffering was above all an inner suffering that cannot be compared with the sufferings of any man, even those of a saint. We have to return to the whole mystery of the divine Son who is a true man if we are to be capable of understanding, in part, all that is contained in the words: "Father, if it is possible, let this cup pass from me" (Mt 26,39). And we have to ponder the whole mystery of this man who is true God if we are to be capable of understanding, in some way, the meaning of St Paul's words: "He who did not spare his own Son but handed him over for us all" (Rom 8,32) and "The one who knew no sin he made to become sin for us" (2 Cor 5,21).

We must now move on from Jesus in his dereliction, his sweat falling like drops of blood. But let us not forget that when he broke off from prayer he said to Peter: "Watch and pray, so that you may not enter into temptation ..." (Mk 14,38).

2. *The second mystery: Jesus is scourged*

The gospel-writers refer only in passing to this appalling laceration of body and spirit: "After having Jesus scourged, he handed him over to them" (Mt 27,26). Historians and biblical scholars have tried to reconstruct the detail of it from other sources. The scourging is the subject of much devotion in Poland, where many hymns written around it are sung in the course of the special Lenten liturgy of compassion for the Lord, known in Polish as "The repentance of grief". "O my Jesus, how cruelly you were bound to the pillar; scourged for our great faults ...". And then in the second part: "For my wickedness the Lord's back is being scourged. Come, you sinners, see – for you is being prepared, in the blood of Jesus, a spring of living water to quench the heart's thirst". Then in the third part of the liturgy, as though it were a lamentation by Our Lady of Sorrows, Polish devotion has her say: "Ah, I see my son, stripped naked against the pillar, scourged with whips ...". The simple words and the gentle melodies, both dating from the 18th century, express very poignantly the sentiments in the hearts of the faithful. The dominant feature of this devotion is its awareness of the close link between that atrocious torture inflicted on Christ's body and mankind's sins of the flesh. The potency of the mystery of the scourging seen in that light is truly remarkable. For many people the scourging of the Lord became the decisive reason for their determination to break the bonds of sin, the reason for mortifying the concupiscence of the flesh, for turning their desires towards the noble and the holy. "I treat my body sternly and keep it under control" (1 Cor 9,27) wrote St Paul, and many others have said the same thing and stressed it by their behaviour. "The flesh has desires that run counter to those of the spirit" (Gal 5,17). "If you live according to the flesh you will die; but if through the spirit you put to death the impulses of the body you will live" (Rom 8,13).

"Ecce hic venit, tinctis vestibus de Bosra" (Is 63,1). Who is the one coming from Bozrah in garments stained with crimson? No doubt we also recall the prophet's subsequent words when in the same context he speaks of the juice that has stained his garments: "torcular calcavi solus – et de gentibus non est vir mecum" – I have trodden the wine-press alone; from all the peoples not one man was with me" (Is 63,3). Let us remember that the Saviour's bloody Passion began when the scourging was inflicted. The flaying at the hands of the soldiers literally drew blood. The maddened crowd shouted: "His blood be upon us and upon our children" (Mt 27,25).

During the Last Supper Jesus said: "This cup is the new

covenant in my blood which is shed for you" (Lk 22,20).
Word and reality. ... And in the book of Revelation St John
was to write: "These are the ones who have washed their
garments and made them white in the blood of the
Lamb ...".

3. *The third mystery: Jesus is crowned with thorns*

The torture inflicted on the Saviour's head was a terrible
one. It is an unforgettable torture, this one chosen by the
soldiers for their mockery of the king of the Jews. The crown
of thorns on the head of the condemned man whom Pilate
had been unable to save from the crowd (cf Mt 27,11–26)
was particularly significant. Pilate had him brought out for
the crowd to see in just that condition, crowned with thorns;
he showed them all his humiliation and said: "Here is the
man" (Jn 19,5).

The significance of those words extends far beyond the
moment in time when they were spoken, and it is far greater
than the one attached to them by the man who spoke them;
there is always meaning to be found in them, far deeper
meaning than they were originally intended to convey. As the
generations and centuries pass there is a development of
understanding of the essential truth they express, a growth
and a deepening of understanding. For the human
intelligence and the human heart are undoubtedly subject to
the laws of development. And the words spoken by Pilate:
"Here is the man" are a case in point.

Pilate knew that Jesus, called the Christ, did not seek here
on earth – least of all in Palestine then under Roman rule –
a kingdom for himself. "My kingdom is not of this world; if
my kingdom were of this world, my defenders would
certainly have fought to prevent me from being handed over
to the Jews; but my kingdom is not an earthly one"
(Jn 18,36). And when Pilate asked the second time, he
received the full explanation: "It is you who say I am a king.
I was born for this, and for this I have come into the world,

to bear witness to the truth. Anyone who loves truth listens to what I have to say" (Jn 18,37).

Here we have before us the Christ in the truth of his kingship. Pilate says: "Here is the man". Precisely. All the kingliness of man, all man's dignity – which Jesus came to express and renew – are here summed up in him. Now it is well known that this is a kingliness that is frequently overpowered, hurled to the ground and thrust deep into the mud. It is also well known that this is a dignity that is subjected to many kinds of humiliation. We are reminded by the second Vatican Council (cf for example, *Lumen gentium*, nn.9,10,26,31,36; *Sacrosanctum Concilium*, n.14; *Presbyterorum ordinis*, n.2; *Apostolicam actuositatem*, nn.2,3; *Ad gentes divinitus*, n.15) that Jesus came in order to reveal the kingliness of man. And here, visible to the whole of humanity, stands Jesus crowned with thorns! The price paid for dignity is the blood of the Son of God!

4. *The fourth mystery: Jesus burdened with the cross climbs Mount Calvary*

In this mystery we are not celebrating the *Via Crucis*, making the stations as we do in Jerusalem or in our churches during Lent. In the fourth sorrowful mystery of the Rosary we try to see the whole of the Lord's *via dolorosa* from one viewpoint only: Jesus burdened with the cross. We visualise him racked with pain, crowned with thorns, his face running with blood and ... burdened with the cross. We see him as "the man of sorrows" (Is 53,3), trampled on by his people, victim of the worst that human cruelty and hatred can devise. And on his shoulders the full weight of the cross! The instrument designed for his own death, the symbol of his dishonour and, above all, a crushing weight. A weight under which he falls. His persecutors themselves have to find someone to help him, someone who with him will carry it to the place of execution. Carrying the weight ... Carrying the cross.... Perhaps at this point we may visualise other men similarly burdened: men held in extermination camps, forced to carry enormous blocks of stone on their shoulders through the quarries; or others harnessed to heavy machinery to do the work of oxen.... The history of the 20th century can by now provide the subjects for many such mental pictures.

Jesus of Nazareth, who carries his cross through the narrow streets of Jerusalem to the place of extermination, has many Simons of Cyrene in our own century, men who – like the Simon of the Gospel – are obliged, often by force, to carry crosses of various kinds. Let us ask ourselves: are they carrying them with Christ?

St Augustine wrote: "amor meus – pondus meum".[1] Here we have, clearly defined, the meaning to be derived from contemplation of the cross of Christ. Love not only uplifts us, takes us out of ourselves; it also lays burdens on us. And perhaps the burdens tell us more about love than do the moments of ecstasy and spiritual élan. "Amor meus – pondus meum". That is why Jesus said: "If anyone wishes to come after me, let him deny himself, take up his cross and follow me" (Mk 8,34). And he said even more: "He who does not take his cross and follow me is not worthy of me" (Mt 10,38). When he spoke those words nobody foresaw that this "great prophet" (cf Lk 7,16) would be burdened with his own cross on which he would die, thus putting the seal on the truth of what he said.

5. *The fifth mystery: Jesus is crucified*

The crucifixion began when the body of Christ was nailed to the wood of the cross; it was a body stripped of clothing, the wounds of the scourging laid bare. They nailed him by the hands and feet. When they levered the cross upright, the whole body hung suspended from the nails driven through the wrists, and the climax of the Passion began. An agony of suffering.... The man who was the Son of God, the "only-begotten", the "beloved" (Mt 3,17; cf 16,16; 17,5 etc; 28,19; Mk 1,1; 12,6...).

Medical analysis of the agony which brought death to an organism that was still young is extremely moving. But no human investigation is capable of reconstructing the mystery of Jesus, who is dying on the cross. We stop still, in silence, on the threshold of all that is most holy in the history of the world. A boundless love, "amor Dei usque ad contemptum sui". Because in this context silence is more eloquent than any words. On Good Friday the Church remains silent. We are silent because we can find no words to fit the occasion. ... If anyone at all has been successful in finding words that are apt – or partially so – it has been saints like Paul, Francis or John of the Cross. But deep silence is best of all, so that the cross itself may speak. *Verbum crucis*, "the language of the cross" (1 Cor 1,18).

Let us briefly recall the words spoken by Christ himself in the agony of his crucifixion:

He said to the Father: "Father, forgive them, for they do not know what they are doing" (Lk 23,34).

He said to one of the thieves: "Truly I say to you, today you shall be with me in paradise" (Lk 23,43).

To his Mother and his disciple he said: "Here is your son Here is your Mother" (Jn 19,26–27).

He said: "I am thirsty" (Jn 19,28).

And then: "Eloi, Eloi, lama sabachthani" (Mk 15,34).

He said: "It is accomplished" (Jn 19,30).

Finally he said with the Psalmist: "Father, into your hands I commend my spirit" (Lk 23,46; Ps 31(30),6).

That said, he gave up his spirit... .

Let us contemplate the Saviour's last words spoken during his agony. They, more than any others, bear witness to his life; they are his testament.

Note

1. *Confessions*, XIII, 9,10.

X.

"Scio enim quod redemptor meus vivit"

---

1. *"Factus est pro nobis oboediens"*

I would like to begin this meditation with some very familiar words. They recur every year at the high point in the Church's liturgy, that is to say when we recall the Lord's passion, death and resurrection. "Christus factus est pro nobis oboediens usque ad mortem" is our chant on Holy Thursday. "Christus factus est pro nobis oboediens usque ad mortem, mortem autem crucis" is how our thoughts proceed on Good Friday. "Propter quod et Deus exaltavit illum et donavit ei nomen quod est super omne nomen" (Phil 2,8–9) is how the Church ends her hymn to the risen Saviour at the Easter Vigil. "Scio enim quod redemptor meus vivit", "But I know that my redeemer lives" (Job 19,25).

I shall never forget what I experienced when, for the first time, I heard those words during the solemn liturgy in the royal cathedral of Wawel in Cracow. I had gone there, still only a youngster, on a Wednesday in Holy Week and stayed for Matins in the early hours. I remember the seminarists seated on their benches, the cathedral canons in their stalls in the choir, and close to the high altar the Archbishop of Cracow, the unforgettable Cardinal Adam Stefan Sapieha. In a central position was a great tripod on which the candles were extinguished one by one as the singing of each psalm came to an end. And finally the chant: "Christus factus est pro nobis oboediens usque ad mortem". After a period of silence, the "Miserere" – Psalm 50, and then the concluding prayer said by the Archbishop: "Respice quaesumus Domine super hanc familiam tuam pro qua Dominus noster Iesus

Christus non dubitavit manibus tradi nocentium et crucis subire tormentum". After which they all departed in total silence.

To this day I often think back to that, because the experience was quite unique; it has never returned with the same intensity, even in the same cathedral, during similar celebrations. It was not merely discovery of the beauty and spiritual attractiveness of the Holy Week liturgy; it was above all discovery of the dimension of the absolute, of the mystery expressed in the liturgy and which the liturgy conveys as a message that is valid for all time.

After St Paul's words concerning Christ's obedience unto death, all present remained perfectly silent, and I felt that not only the men but the whole cathedral itself was preserving that silence, that cathedral on which my country's history is centred.

The whole of humanity, the Church and the world, the past, the present and the future all come together in the deepest silence, full of adoration, before the fact that "Christus factus est pro nobis oboediens usque ad mortem". Silent adoration is the human spirit's most fitting response, its "right word" par excellence. Silence in the presence of the mystery by which God, through his Son who was obedient unto death, accomplishes the great work of justification, bringing the mystery of redemption into the mystery of creation. Thus in the dimension of the truth and justice of God the mystery of creation reaches completion. "Indeed my thoughts are not your thoughts, and your ways are not my ways, says the Lord. As high as the heavens are above the earth, so far do my ways surpass your ways, and my thoughts surpass your thoughts" (Is 55,8–9).

The mystery of redemption infinitely surpasses the thoughts and the ways of men. It is a divine mystery in which God expresses his own self – his justice and mercy, his holiness which is love. "God is love", wrote St John (1 Jn 4,8.16). At the same time through this mystery the God of infinite majesty expresses his attitude towards the world, the universe and man in particular. This mystery of God derives from the whole history of man and of the world. It springs from the conflict between the Word and the anti-Word, between Love and anti-Love. In this mystery the "amor Dei usque ad contemptum sui" confronts the "amor sui usque ad contemptum Dei".[1] And this mystery of salvation, flowing as it does from the heart and the sacrifice of the divine man of history, takes shape in an historical event; but although it occurs within time, in its inner meaning it transcends time and reaches a dimension that is divine and at the same time human.

St Paul delves even more deeply into this reality – which has a cosmic dimension though above all an anthropological one – when he writes: "Therefore as sin entered the world through one man – and, because of sin, death – and thus death spread to all men because all sinned ... . Therefore as one man's fall led to condemnation for all men, so one man's work of justice leads to justification and life for all. For as through one man's disobedience many were made sinners, so by one man's obedience many will be made just" (Rom 5,12–19).

The antithesis is very clear: disobedience-obedience, sinners-the just. "Christ became obedient unto death". What is meant by obedience? There are many different concepts and understandings of obedience. It always entails accepting the will of a superior, a higher will. But the motives for acceptance, and the manner of acceptance, can vary a great deal. There can be blind obedience, or there can be unwilling obedience, given under coercion, and this – because of the attitude of mind and the intention – more closely resembles disobedience.

Obedience and disobedience both stem from the will, from freedom: will and freedom face to face with the divine will. When St Paul contrasts the disobedience of the first Adam with the obedience of the second Adam, Christ, both have to be seen in their full dimensions. The full dimension of the obedience of Christ is determined by the Word and by Love, just as the disobedience of the first man has its source in the anti-Word and anti-Love. The Word speaks the truth about God, who is Father (cf Jn 6,27), Love (1 Jn 4,8.16); and, working with God, instils love. This truth and this love find expression in the obedience of Jesus, his "obedience unto death". That was the transcendental response to the disobedience of mankind, in which the "father of lies" played a part (Jn 8,44) together with the anti-Love generated by the lies.

The Son's obedience to the Father also does justice to the God of infinite majesty who at the same time is the God of the covenant. From the very dawn of history injustice has made itself at home in the world: men, communities, nations have all treated one another unjustly. Holy scripture is full of repeated appeals to men to live and work as justice requires. Yet in spite of that, injustice stalks mankind throughout history.

Even today! Our age is full to overflowing with the most heartrending examples of injustice. The 1971 Synod of Bishops drew attention to this among other things. Today the world echoes with a desperate cry for social justice, for justice as it affects each and every man. How much injustice there is today, parading under the banner of justice! It is becoming ever more clear that the achievement of a just society, a just world, is a task that confronts every man in every age.

Jesus Christ took upon himself the burden of this problem and solved it by going to the root of it. Man first became unjust when he became disobedient to the Creator. For that reason Christ became obedient unto death, thus bequeathing to mankind his own justice to serve as an inexhaustible fount of justification before God. In the past, and even to this day, there have been so many programmes promising "healing" for the world and proclaiming the arrival of "true" justice in men's dealings with one another. But none of these can be regarded as complete unless it is linked with the justification before God – which is the main foundation of all justice –

that we attain thanks to the obedience of Christ, obedience unto death ... .

2. *Redemption*

Jesus Christ goes forward to meet death, death on the cross. He goes forward to meet those who have come to the garden of olives to arrest him on the High Priest's orders. "Whom do you seek?". They answer: "Jesus the Nazarene". "I have told you that I am he", replies Jesus, "so, if I am the one you seek, let these others go away" (Jn 18,7). And at that moment there began the great event to which humanity constantly refers. We all remember how Vatican II dealt with the question of responsibility for Jesus's death, his condemnation first in the High Priest's palace and then in Pilate's praetorium. After two thousand years the Council finally made clear how the Church sees the problem of this responsibility.

As the old man Simeon bent over the tiny child who had been brought to the temple of Jerusalem, he prophesied that Jesus would be "a sign of contradiction" (cf Lk 2,34). These words were applicable to Jesus throughout his life, and they can still be applied to him now, as we saw when we began this retreat.

But let us now ask ourselves a question: was Jesus himself really a man full of contradictions? There has never been, either in the past or in our own day, any shortage of people who see him above all as a revolutionary, and try to adapt the various concepts and philosophies of revolution so as to make them fit in with the basic meaning and purpose of Christianity.[2] Yet any objective examination of the Gospel shows Jesus Christ to have been above all a teacher of truth and a servant of love; and it is these characteristics of his which explain the real meaning of all that he did and all that he set out to do. They also explain both the "contradiction" inherent in his mission and activities and the "contradiction"

aroused by the teaching and behaviour of the teacher from
Nazareth (cf Jn 1,45).

Jesus disputed the totally mistaken and false inter-
pretations of the word of God and the tradition of the chosen
people that were upheld by the Pharisees and Sadducees. He
opposed whatever was not in keeping with the primary and
fundamental truth of the Word. He opposed all the petty
human meannesses that were distorting the Law and the
greatest of all the commandments, the law of love. He
opposed them not only in what he said but in what he did.
His teaching consisted above all in the works he performed:
"... all that Jesus began to do and teach" (Acts 1,1). He
never intended this opposition, this "contradiction", to have
any political implication: "Give back to Caesar the things
that are Caesar's and to God the things that are God's"
(Mt 22,21; Lk 20,25).

"Non arripit terrena qui regna dat celestia", is the
Church's chant on the feast of Epiphany.

Jesus the Christ went forward towards death in full
awareness of his messianic destiny. He knew that the destiny
of all humanity and the whole world lay with him and his
cross. Scourged, mocked with a crown of thorns, he carried
to Mount Calvary together with the weight of his cross the
truth of human suffering, humiliation, scorn, torture, agony,
death. Albert Camus has written that he was always on the
side of the powerless, the socially disadvantaged (cf Jn 7,49).
On the day of his death Jesus entered into the fullest and
deepest communion and solidarity with the entire human
family, and especially with all those who throughout history
have been the victims of injustice, cruelty and scornful abuse.
And in shouldering all this in his true human nature, he, the
sign of contradiction, was above all the "lamb of God who
takes away the sin of the world" (Jn 1,29). That is how John
the Baptist described him on the bank of the Jordan; and
that is what he is in the life of the People of God. The Lamb
of God, the paschal sacrifice (1 Cor 5,7; Ex 11,5–7), a

reminder of past deliverance and a promise of deliverance to come.

The cross was an instrument of torture and disgrace for the man condemned (cf Mk 15,27; Jn 19,17; Gal 5,11). The cross was a chosen sign (Phil 2,8–9; Gal 6,14; 1 Cor 1,18). In it the vertical and the horizontal meet; it is thus an expression of the most profound interaction of the divine and the human.

It is at this point of intersection, symbolic but also real, that we find the sacrificial Lamb of God, the God-man.

Jesus embraced all things in order to restore all things to his Father. And by this act of restitution, this act of sacrifice, he has made all things "new" (cf Jer 31,31).

"Ecce nova facio omnia" ... . This is the point in history when all men are so to speak "conceived" afresh and follow a new course within God's plan – the plan prepared by the Father in the truth of the Word and in the gift of Love. It is the point at which the history of mankind makes a fresh start, no longer dependent on human conditioning – if one may put it like that. This fresh starting-point belongs in the divine order of things, in the divine perspective on man and the world. The finite, human categories of time and space are almost completely secondary. All men, from the beginning of the world until its end, have been redeemed by Christ and his cross.

3. *"Won back for God by a shedding of blood"*

All this was effected through a shedding of blood (cf Heb 9,12). Let us now link the historical picture handed down to us by the gospel-writers – the cross, Calvary, the crucified Christ – with another, the one drawn by St John in the fifth chapter of Revelation: "And I saw in the right hand of the one seated on the throne a scroll with writing inside and seven seals on the outside. And I saw a powerful angel who called in a loud voice: Who is worthy to open the scroll and break the seals? But no-one in heaven or on the earth or under the earth was able to open the scroll or look into it. I wept bitterly because no-one could be found who was worthy to open the scroll and look inside it. But one of the elders said to me: Do not weep. Look, the Lion of the tribe of Judah, the Root of David, has conquered, so that he can open the scroll and break its seven seals. Then I looked, and I saw between the throne and the four living creatures a Lamb standing .... He came and took the scroll from the right hand of the one seated on the throne .... And they sang a new song, saying: You are worthy to take the scroll and open its seals because you were slain and have won us back for God from every tribe and language and people and nation, and you have made us kings and priests for our God, and we shall reign over the earth" (Rev 5,1–10).

He won us back for God by shedding his blood! We all belong to God (cf 1 Cor 3,22–23), everything belongs to God, by virtue of creation. But for the eternal Truth and the eternal Love that was not enough. It did not accord fully with the divine economy, especially after the fall of man prompted by the rebellious spirit – the fallen angel. Above all it was not enough once the workings of the anti-Word and anti-Love had made inroads into creation and human history. It was not enough! We all needed to be "won back" "reclaimed by a payment in blood", "redeemed".

Was the shedding of that particular blood really necessary? Why the blood of Jesus? Why the cross? For centuries past these questions have been asked. They recur time and again in the lines of the poets and the speculations of the philosophers. They are still being asked by the men of our day. The mystery of the cross cannot be fully assessed by approaching it from one angle alone, by studying it by one method alone. The mystery implicit in the cross is far beyond man's intellectual grasp, far beyond human understanding. Yet it constantly recurs whenever man reflects on the world, on God, on himself, on good and evil, on eternity. And always we find fresh aspects of the ineffable mystery to contemplate. "Stat crux, dum volvitur orbis". In his first letter to the Corinthians St Paul set out the truth of the divine transcendence of the cross when he wrote: "... while the Jews ask for miracles and the Greeks seek wisdom, we preach Christ crucified, a stumbling-block to the Jews and folly to the pagans; but for those who are called, Jews as well as Greeks, Christ is the power of God, the wisdom of God, because the folly of God is wiser than men and the weakness of God is stronger than men" (1,22–25). In the cross there lies, concealed, power to redeem the world and justify men before God; but in the cross another power too lies concealed, and therefore another meaning. How often man turns to God to confront him with demands! God is expected to relieve sufferings, to correct injustices, even to put an end to all the world's evil. But when a man turns his eyes to the cross, his thoughts make an abrupt about-turn. It's very strange: it's as if the one hanging from the cross, Jesus, had justified everything; it's as if at that moment – *ut minus sapiens dico* – he had justified God himself before man.[3] This is also one particular manifestation of the covenant, in that it is a shining example of the divine condescension. Thus the truth of the cross goes to the very heart of reality, penetrates all the dimensions of good and evil that have developed in the course of human and world history.

In the truth of the cross there lies also, *perfectum opus laudis*, adoration of the God of infinite majesty, adoration of a quality and intensity that no created being, no matter how perfect, has ever been capable of expressing. In the cross lies Love's victory: "Amor Dei usque ad contemptum sui". In it, finally, lies the full truth about man, man's true stature, his wretchedness and his grandeur, his worth and the price paid for him. "God loved the world so much that he sacrificed his only Son" (Jn 3,16).

"But I know that my avenger lives ...": "Scio enim quod redemptor meus vivit ..." (Job 19,25).

Redemption is the nucleus of the paschal mystery so often remembered by the second Vatican Council in so many different contexts. In that mystery the Church rediscovered the key to solving, in Christ, all the most difficult problems facing man and the world.

Notes

1. St Augustine, *De civitate Dei*, xiv, 28.
2. Cf Hans Küng, *Christ sein*, Munich-Zurich 1974.
3. John Milton, *Paradise lost*, I, 22.

XI.

The Bridegroom is with you

---

1. *The great jubilee*

"The Church believes that Christ, who died and rose again for all men, always gives to man, through his Spirit, light and strength to respond to his supreme vocation; nor have men been given any other name on earth by which they can be saved. She also believes that in her Lord and Master are to be found the key, the focal point and the goal of mankind and of all human history. The Church also affirms that beneath everything that is subject to change lie realities that are immutable; these have their ultimate foundation in Christ who is the same yesterday, today and for ever". Those are the words of the Pastoral Constitution *Gaudium et spes*, n. 10.

Thus the birth of the Church, at the time of the messianic and redemptive death of Christ, coincided with the birth of "the new man" – whether or not man was aware of such a rebirth and whether or not he accepted it. At that moment man's existence acquired a new dimension, very simply expressed by St Paul as "in Christ" (cf Rom 6,23; 8,39; 12,5; 15,17; 16,7 and other letters).

Man exists "in Christ", and he had so existed from the beginning in God's eternal plan; but it is by virtue of Christ's death and resurrection that this "existence in Christ" became historical fact, with roots in time and space. That being so, we are right to begin the count of the years from the year of Christ's birth, we are right to try by means of the liturgical calendar to bring within the framework of time the whole divine dimension of the Incarnation and Redemption, and we are right to celebrate every 25 years the great jubilee known as the Holy Year.

Birth is always a beginning, a looking towards the future. The birth of the Church as the new man "in Christ" and the new people "in Christ" is inextricably bound up with the Redeemer's death on the cross. In one sense that beginning is more like the Church's conception than her birth. The birth took place when what had been conceived on the cross was revealed to the world. That is why tradition very rightly looks on Pentecost as the day when the Church was born. But that birth really began on Mount Calvary, even though there was no external manifestation of it. Just as the child exists in the mother's womb from the moment of conception but becomes fully visible only at birth – even its mother cannot see it until then although she had carried it and felt it in her womb – so the Mother of Christ, whom the Holy Father has called "Mother of the Church",[1] was first able at Pentecost to see her Son reborn in his new body which is the Church.

When the Holy Father proclaimed the Holy Year at this latter end of the century, we realised that in accordance with centuries-old tradition we were to celebrate afresh the great jubilee of Christ's marriage to the Church, effected by his own death and resurrection.

We all celebrate our own personal jubilees: for a married couple their mutual promise of fidelity, for a priest his total dedication of himself to Christ, and so on. The Church looks back in a very special way to the time of her birth and simultaneous marriage to the divine bridegroom. This she does every 25 years, and she did so again in 1975. We all know that there was opposition of various kinds to the idea. Some expressed the view that the Holy Year was an outmoded institution and that to give it a fresh lease of life would be contrary to the ecumenical spirit of the times. Other objections and difficulties were raised during the jubilee year itself. But in spite of all that we did celebrate the Holy Year again in 1975, and that was important in itself. As it ran its course it confirmed the rightness of the decision that welled up within the heart of the Pope – the decision to lay once again before all people the mystery of the Holy Year in all its meaning, christological, pneumatological, mariological, ecclesiological and ecumenical.

The Holy Year provided the opportunity for a great coming-together of the whole of the post-conciliar Church; it was an opportunity to give fresh impetus to the work of renewal and reconciliation. And throughout all the many different activities – pilgrimages, audiences, conferences, canonisations, beatifications, prayer and penitence – there seemed to echo one cry: "The Bridegroom is with you!". And the Church heard it and understood: Christ is with us, the Bridegroom is with us! He is with the Church, he is with every man, woman and child, he is with the entire human family.

How then can the Bridegroom's friends fail to remember that he is present, and fail to think back to the days of that birth and death which have shaped their whole lives? Such recollection is more necessary than ever at the present time when attempts are being made to desacralise the whole of human life, to break all its closest ties with Christianity, to sever its link with the living God, the indissoluble link forged with every human person and with the entire human race through Christ's liberating death and resurrection.

2. *Eucharist*

On the day of Pentecost the Apostles understood the meaning of the words they had heard in the upper room on the eve of their Master's death: "It is better for you that I should go away; because if I do not go away the comforter will not come to you; but if I do go I shall send him to you" (Jn 16,7). ... "But when he, the Spirit of truth, has come, he will guide you towards the whole truth" (Jn 16,13). These words came true in the upper room on the day of Pentecost. The Apostles began to speak that same truth in different languages, and this came about by virtue of an inner power deep in their souls. From that moment they preached the Gospel as Christ himself had preached it – "like one who has authority" (Mt 7,29). Moreover that inner spiritual power was to communicate itself to others who would be converted thanks to their preaching. In his nocturnal talk with the Lord, Nicodemus had asked with some incredulity: "How can a man be re-born when he is old?" (Jn 3,4). And now, on the very day the Church was born, several thousand people who listened to the Apostles received baptism. The work of evangelisation had begun, as the Lord had commanded: "Go out into the whole world and preach the Gospel to all creation. Whoever believes and is baptised will be saved" (Mk 16,15–16).

All of that flowed from the death of Christ, from his pierced side, in full accord with what he himself had said: "Unless a grain of seed falls to the ground and dies it remains a single grain; but if it dies it bears much fruit" (Jn 12,24).

So now, not only "mors et vita duello conflixere mirando" – in the words of the old Easter Day sequence – but death became the beginning of life, the abundant source of new life (cf Rom 5,17; 1 Cor 15,21). This is the substance of the divine mystery which gives life to the Church and to humanity.

The death of Jesus Christ on the cross is an act of supreme love: "amor Dei usque ad contemptum sui". It is in character with the love both of the Redeemer and of the Bridegroom. On Holy Thursday Jesus said to the Apostles: "I am going away ... and I shall come back to you ..." (Jn 14,3; 14,18). By the day of Pentecost the Apostles undoubtedly perceived the meaning of those words: Christ had returned: or rather he had always remained with them. They suddenly became aware that the Church was a reality; and this awareness was due not only to that "power from on high" (Lk 24,49) which Jesus had promised at the time of the Ascension: "... with the coming of the Holy Spirit you will receive the inner power to become witnesses to me"

(Acts 1,8), but also to the power that Jesus had placed in the hands of the Apostles on Holy Thursday when he said: "Do this in memory of me" (Lk 22,19; 1 Cor 11,24). The Apostles were then in the upper room, as they were on the day of Pentecost too. He took the bread, broke it and gave it to them saying: "This is my body, offered in sacrifice for you" (1 Cor 11,24). And then: "This is the cup of my blood for the new and everlasting covenant, shed for you and for all men ..." (cf Lk 22,20). Thus he spoke on the eve of his Passion, before his body had been offered in sacrifice, before his blood had been shed. And he added: "Do this ...". This he himself did as he broke the bread, as he offered them the wine in the cup, as he spoke the words. This he himself did, and he said to them; "*Do* this". Thus he forged the link between his own action and their actions. The link he forged lasts for ever. Thus he perpetuated what was signified by the action he carried out in the upper room. And what was signified by that action was made plain for all to see the following day: the body had been offered in sacrifice and the blood had been shed. The cross and death.

"We proclaim your death, Lord, we proclaim your resurrection as we await your coming" is the people's response when an Apostle's hands – and then other consecrated hands – perform those same actions, in memory of him.

"See, I am with you for all time until the end of the world" (Mt 28,20). ... "I am going away ... and I shall come back to you" (Jn 14,3). "I am ...", but not merely as a memory, as someone written and talked about. "I am", I am present in the sacrament of my death, that death through which I went away from you. I continually go away and come back through that same death. I am: "vere, substantialiter, sacramentaliter" (DS 883/1651). I am ... the power of the Holy Spirit, the power from on high that shapes and sustains the Church, the community of the People of God. The Church's principal means of sustenance is this sacramental action of the Eucharist in which the sacrifice

and the constant presence of the Saviour are manifested to
the faithful. Our preparation for this sacrament – so fittingly
called the Eucharist – is Baptism, the sacrament by which
we were "buried" in the death and resurrection of Christ (cf
Rom 6,3–11).

3. *The Church: the body and the bride*

Christ's presence in the Church – his eucharistic, sacramental and at the same time charismatic presence – shows that
his "going away" in death is the immediate cause of his
"coming back" in the dimension of the Gift, the uncreated
everlasting Gift which is none other than the Holy Spirit
(Jn 15,26). And this "coming back" by Christ in the Holy
Spirit – on the day of Pentecost and to this day – has the
character of the return of the Bridegroom.

It is a "bestowal", a divinely generous bestowal. No other
view of it is possible. When the Church celebrates the great
sacrament of the body and blood of Christ, Christ bestows on
each and every member of the Church not only himself but
himself in the mystery of redemption and justification. He
gives himself in the full reality of the new life. This is a gift
of his Person and of his action, that conclusive, definitive,
redemptive and therefore saving action. "Do this in memory
of me" (Lk 22,19; 1 Cor 11,24). It is a gift that expresses
love, not only the love of the Lamb of God on the cross:
"amor Dei usque ad contemptum sui", but also the love of
the Bridegroom, for whom the Church – and also every
human soul "in Christ" – becomes a bride. Consequently,
the Church takes shape in a new dimension: "in Christ".

We know that this figure of speech was used in the Old
Testament to express the love of God for his people: the
metaphor of bridegroom and bride often recurs in the
writings of prophets like Hosea, Isaiah, Jeremiah and
Ezekiel. Jesus himself used it only once, almost as if by
accident, when he said: "Can the bridegroom's friends fast
while the bridegroom is with them?" (Mk 2,19). But even-

tually it reached full development in St Paul's ecclesiology, in his letter to the Ephesians:

"Let wives be subject to their husbands as if to the Lord because the husband is the head of the wife just as Christ is the head of the Church, he, the saviour of the body. And as the Church is subject to Christ, so wives should be subject to their husbands in everything. And you, husbands, love your wives as Christ loved the Church and sacrificed himself for her, to sanctify her, purifying her with the baptism of water and in the strength of the word, so that he might present her to himself in all her glory, without spot or wrinkle or anything of the kind, and so that she might be holy and unblemished. Thus husbands must love their wives as their own bodies. He who loves his wife loves himself. Nobody ever hates his own body but feeds it and cares for it as Christ feeds and cares for the Church, for we are members of Christ's body. For this reason a man is to leave his father and mother and be one with his wife, and the two are to be one flesh. This is a great mystery, but I am speaking about the relationship between Christ and the Church ..." (5,22–32).

St Paul is in fact speaking about two relationships, both of them essential: Christ is head of the Church which is his body, and Christ is the bridegroom of the Church which is his bride. These two relationships are, however, closely linked with one another in the Apostle's thought when he writes: "husbands must love their wives as their own bodies". Starting from this principle we can perceive in the passage quoted the truth concerning the bridegroom-like love which characterises the relationship between Christ and Church: "Christ loved the Church and sacrificed himself for her, to sanctify her, purifying her with the baptism of water and in the strength of the word, so that he might present her to himself in all her glory, without spot or wrinkle or anything of the kind ...". It is the love of husbands and wives, in which there is mutual self-giving and the fruit of that self-giving; it is a real bestowal. In the relationship between

Christ and the Church, Christ bestows purification, sanctification, grace and all the joys of salvation.

So the love of Christ-the-Bridegroom stems directly from
the cross and the sacrifice. The Redeemer is the Bridegroom
by virtue of being the Redeemer! He is able to bring his Gift
to the Church precisely because he has already given himself
in the sacrifice of his blood.

The Eucharist is, in its turn, the sacrament of this Gift,
the principal source of all that is bestowed on the Church
and on all men. It is inexhaustible in its riches which pulsate
"in Christ". It is Christ himself, mediator of the perfect
covenant, the new and everlasting covenant with the Father,
and mediator of the full bestowal – on men and on the world
– of the Holy Spirit: "Spiritus Domini replevit orbem
terrarum et hoc, quod continet omnia, scientiam habet vocis"
(Entrance antiphon, Pentecost, Wis 1,7).

What is bestowed cannot be seen, for its dimension is that
of man's inner life. Yet it has its own form of expression:
"scientiam habet vocis". And just as it found expression in
the words of St Peter on the day of Pentecost, so it always
seeks to make itself evident through the Church, through all
that is done by the successor of Peter, by the successors of
the other Apostles, and by the whole People of God, priests,
laity, religious. More than ever nowadays there is a need for
such a manifestation, one that is strong, authentic and suited
to the times – as was the first one on the day of Pentecost.
All invocation of the Spirit, all emphasis on the "pneumatological" such as was clearly evident during the 1974 Synod
of Bishops, is in fact invocation of Christ himself as
Redeemer and Bridegroom. "And the Spirit and the Bride
say: Come!", wrote St John (Rev 22,17; cf 1 Cor 16,22).

I think that the mystery of the Holy Spirit at work in the
life of the Church was greatly enhanced, above all pastorally,
by the Holy Year. You are all familiar with what took place
here, in Rome, during that great event of 1975; but I think
that our experiences in Poland, especially in 1974, are worth
remembering too. In Poland we were all very conscious of the

fact that the Holy Year was a time when the Church's divine Bridegroom wished to offer us a special gift. So it was up to us to see that we were well prepared for receiving it. In 1974 the Bishops – as the Bridegroom's servants – visited every parish, not only to celebrate the Holy Year with the parish communities but also to prepare the way for the divine Bridegroom, for his special Holy Year gift. And I really must say that, considering all the spiritual benefit we derived by God's grace from the years 1974 and 1975, our hopes were certainly not disappointed. One particular sign that the Lord was offering us a gift was the high number of candidates – higher than ever – applying to enter the seminaries. Thanks be to Christ and his Mother.

"Christ loved the Church and sacrificed himself for her" (Eph 5,27). We must always see the Church as she is in the reality of her existence in history. The Church is the People of God, that is to say she is man – both as person and as community – living "in Christ" according to the standard so clearly but profoundly set out by the second Vatican Council: "... the Lord Jesus, when he prayed to the Father 'that all may be one as we are one' (Jn 17,21–22) offered us possibilities unforeseen by human reasoning. For he implied a certain similarity between the union of the divine Persons and the union of God's children in truth and charity. This similarity shows clearly that man, the only creature on earth that God willed for its own sake, cannot fully find himself except by sincerely giving himself" (*Gaudium et spes*, n. 24).

Thus the Council teaches us – and this teaching is at the heart of its magisterium – that "only in the mystery of the incarnate Word is light shed on the mystery of man" (*Gaudium et spes*, n. 22). We therefore propose to consider more fully, in our forthcoming meditations, this great mystery of man: "in Christ".

Really there does seem to be a need to recall and repeat to the men of our day: the Bridegroom is with you! His love for you is so great that he gave himself fully and irrevocably. Jesus wished us to inherit from him nothing less than love of every single human being. It may seem a poor inheritance, but in fact its potential is immense. For what else does man seek except to be loved? What else gives human existence its fundamental meaning? We are poor, but we are rich. The Bridegroom is with you!

Note

1. Address of Pope Paul VI, 21st November 1964.

XII.

Christ "fully reveals man to man himself"[1]

As I said at the end of the last meditation, the love of Christ who "loved the Church and sacrificed himself for her", the love of the Bridegroom, goes out to every human being. This truth is central to the second Vatican Council's Pastoral Constitution on "The Church in the world of today". One particular text that we must always take into account has provoked widespread comment and given rise to a great deal of very profound thought, both theological and pastoral. It is section 22 of the Constitution, at the end of the first chapter entitled "The dignity of the human person". Let us read a passage from it:

"The fact is that only in the mystery of the incarnate Word is light shed on the mystery of man. Adam, the first man, pre-figured the man to come (Rom 5,14), Christ the Lord. Christ, who is the new Adam, by revealing the mystery of the Father and his love, also fully reveals man to man himself and makes his exalted vocation known to him. It is therefore no wonder that all the truths set out above flow from Christ and reach their highest form of expression in him. He is the image of the unseen God (Col 1,15), he is the perfect man, who has restored to the children of Adam the likeness to God which was distorted at the very beginning by sin. Because he assumed human nature without in any way destroying it, human nature in us too has by that very fact been raised to a dignity that is sublime. By the Incarnation the Son of God united himself in some way with every man. He worked with human hands, he thought with a human mind .... By being born of the Virgin Mary he made

himself truly one of us, like us in all things but sin"
(*Gaudium et spes*, n. 22).

As the meaning of that text is very clear, there is no need
to examine every word of it; but let us try to pick out what
seems new and inspiring in it:

First: The concept of the mystery of man, taken in
conjunction with the fact of man's being "revealed" to man
himself, clearly has something to say to two current schools
of thought. On the one hand, rationalism and empiricism
have led – and still try to do so – to the belief that man is
nothing more than an object for scientific investigation; while
on the other hand that same sort of belief has in turn led to
an awareness that man is an 'unknown' being, "L'homme,
cet inconnu", to quote Carrel. The category of mystery could
hardly be more applicable.

Second: By applying the category of mystery to man, the
conciliar text makes clear the anthropological, even anthropocentric character of the revelation offered to mankind in
Christ. This revelation is centred on man: Christ "fully
reveals man to man himself". But he does so by revealing the
Father and the Father's love (cf Jn 17,6).

Third: This revelation is no theory or ideology. It consists
in a fact – the fact that by his incarnation the Son of God
united himself with every man, became man himself, one of
us: "like us in all things except sin" (Heb 4,15). Jesus lived
an authentic human life, and we know that the difficulties he
encountered were such as to make him always and for ever
close to all who have to endure trials and sufferings in their
own lives.

Fourth: Finally: the incarnation of the Son of God
emphasises the great dignity of human nature; and the
mystery of redemption not only reveals the value of every
human being but also indicates the lengths to which the
battle to save man's dignity must go.

There we have the essentials of the Council's teaching –
which is therefore the Church's teaching – on man and the

mystery of man, a mystery which can be finally and fully explained in Christ alone.

A book entitled *"Who is Jesus Christ for me?"* was published in Cracow in 1975. It contains the results of an investigation, in the form of a questionnaire, mounted by a Catholic weekly that for 30 years has concentrated on socio-cultural matters; as such it is almost unique in Poland. Hundreds of replies to the questionnaire were received. Reproduced in the book under various subject headings they provide a most impressive picture of many people's inner lives. As a bishop and pastor I was greatly moved when I read the book, for every reply brought confirmation of the fundamental importance – for the Church and for Christianity – of the truth about the Person of Christ, alive in men, in their thoughts and in their hearts. Who is Jesus Christ for these people? All the replies received by the editors were anonymous, but nonetheless they all had the flavour of true confessions, because they disclosed deep spiritual problems arising out of the correspondents' own religious and moral experience. Anonymity was of course a prerequisite for sincerity and honesty. And the sincerity and honesty of those replies showed me, as a bishop and pastor, how grace indeed abounds; and they showed me, too, the nature of the "love of Christ that surpasses all knowledge" (Eph 3,19).

Let me tell you a little more about this book, which runs to nearly 400 pages. Among the writers are young and old alike, cultured people and simple people; but the cultured are more numerous, and this affects the style of the book's comments. The vast majority are laity, and people facing difficulties of one kind or another. Most are believers; but some replies came from waverers or outright non-believers.

The list of headings is in itself informative. To the question: "Who is Jesus Christ for you?", one young worker's reply can be summed up as: "He was one of us"; and that means a great deal. The young usually reply very briefly: "He permeates my whole life", "I know that he loves me", "I see him in every human being", "He has taught me how to love", "My Christ is the one who listens and answers", "I grow to understand him from what I find in other men", "Christ is life – and these are not just fine words". Similar replies can be found throughout the book: "Mystery", "A perfect example of man", "The most human of men", "A friend", "The Christ of peace", "He is now everything for me", "The one who is waiting for me", "The one who commands by the example he sets", "The one who guides me", "The one I trust", "A guide and an authority", "Presence", "Meaning and purpose", "Boundless mercy", "Hope and mystery", "A concrete reality", "He is happiness", "He just is".

Here is one more: "For me Christ is a supreme Love that awaits, forgives and embraces all men without exception"; the writer was a man of 28, a university lecturer.

One seminarist wrote: "I am very glad to be able to say something about the Christ in my life ... . I believe that one cannot be a complete man without Christ. That is Christ for me, the answer to what is most important of all ... . I want to shout for joy because I, a man, can be born again in God. That is why I celebrate the day of your Nativity as if it were my own birthday; for you have given me complete confidence in my human nature ... Love. Nowadays we are very cautious about using the word. But I intend to use it: Christ, the greatest of all the Creator's loves, God's marriage to us".

A lawyer stressed the need for continually choosing in favour of Christ: "I am infinitely grateful to my divine guide, my anchor of truth, who is so relevant to our times. I try always to have in mind the Master's words: 'Nobody can serve two masters; for either he will despise the one and love the other, or he will become attached to the one and lose sight of the other'. It is this firm statement that enables me to keep my self-respect, to be myself in my work, at home, among my friends and acquaintances. I continually thank the God-man for that; because it means that I am always free, at any time and in any place, to worship him unceasingly, regardless of whether the worship is public or private".

Many correspondents admit quite frankly that for them Christ is not easy to accept. "It is not enough to say just once in life: I will believe! One has to go on saying it again and again, whenever things get difficult. Difficulties do arise, times when one has to take up the cross daily. And then Christ is not easy to accept, but he is truer than ever. ... When I bow to this truth I feel myself a pupil of a really wonderful Master. Too often I look at Christ with the eyes of 'this world'. Often I think that the two thousand years that have gone by are an insuperable barrier, and I forget that God is not bound by time but comes at all times, and always comes in search of his creature – man. That having once come he comes all the time, even today. Jesus, true God and true man, is there before me all the time with his amazing suggestion that I should put my trust in him, whatever may happen tomorrow or next year or at the end ... without fear, without grumbling. Confide in him about everything. ... He helps 'for today', and all these 'todays' add up to years. When I find it difficult to connect God's coming two thousand years ago with his coming now, today, nothing helps more than to go to him in the Eucharist believing what he said: 'I am with you to the end of the world'. This daily act of faith opens the door to grace, which sustains my faith. Grace and my own will collaborate; it is wonderful. I believe that this is what God wanted for man, the joy of choosing God, the choice that suffering teaches us to make. ... May those who are capable of understanding understand! ...".

Since this "anthropological" meditation has led us into the realm of man's deepest thoughts, opinions and convictions concerning the person of Christ, perhaps I may be allowed to recall yet another one. The Polish association of atheists and freethinkers produces a weekly paper which, in 1965, printed an article by Leszek Kolakowski entitled "Jesus Christ, prophet and reformer". The author is a fairly well-known professor of philosophy who for some years now has been

living outside Poland. In his article Kolakowski does his best
to maintain a completely neutral attitude towards the various
individual forms that christian belief can take; he is not
concerned with dogma or with membership of any ecclesial
community – although his article certainly is not free of
"anti-ecclesial" and "anti-clerical" observations. All the
same, Kolakowski asserts that the various attempts that have
been made to eradicate Jesus from our culture merely
because "we do not believe in the God he believed in" are
ridiculous and absurd. "Any such attempts – he wrote – are
the work of people so ingenuous as to imagine that atheism
pure and simple is not only perfectly adequate as *weltanschauung* but also justifies mutilating our cultural tradition
so as to make it accord with atheism's own doctrinaire view,
thus severing that tradition from its roots". Kolakowski bases
his position on a conviction that quite independently of
religion or Church there exist in world culture, especially in
European culture, certain fundamental values and meanings
that derive from Christ alone. This is how he ends: "It is not
possible, without breaking the continuity of the life of the
spirit, to plunge into 'non-being' the person of that man who
for centuries was ... an example of the highest values: he
proved himself capable of forthrightly expressing his own
truth, of uncompromisingly defending it all the way, of
resisting to the very end the pressures of the establishment
which refused to accept him. He taught how one can face up
to oneself and to the world without resorting to violence.
Thus he was an example of that radical authenticity to which
every human being can, with his or her own values, truly
devote his or her life". Among the values for which world
culture is indebted to Christianity Kolakowski lists five as
being of great importance: the supplanting of law in favour
of love; the ideal of an end to arrogance in human relationships; the truth that man does not live by bread alone; the
abolition of the idea of the chosen people (Kolakowski
interprets that as meaning that no longer are there any
nations with a right, for any reason, to impose their rule on

others); and finally the proposition that the world suffers from an organic imperfection.

From all that we have been considering it is clear that the one big question concerning Christ has constantly been asked, by Christians and non-Christians, believers and non-believers. Having listened to various testimonies based on lived experience, perhaps we would now do well to recall the very first time that question was asked, and the answer it was then given – the most accurate answer of all. The question was first asked by Jesus himself, and he put it to his own followers, the Apostles: "Who do people say the Son of man is?" (Mt 16,13). The answer came from the lips of the first Pope: "You are the Christ, the Son of the living God" (Mt 16,16). Let us remember the words with which the Lord confirmed the truth of that reply. We are well aware how central to the Church, to this day, is that endorsement of Peter's faith: "Blessed are you, Simon son of Jonah, for this has been revealed to you not by flesh and blood but by my Father who is in heaven. And I say to you that you are Peter, and on this rock I shall build my Church, and the gates of hell will never prevail against it. And to you I shall give the keys of the kingdom of heaven: whatever you bind on earth will be bound in heaven, and whatever you loose on earth will be loosed in heaven" (Mt 16,17–19).

The Church is centred on Peter and his faith, and that centre is a visible one. But we have to remember that Peter's affirmation was made in reply to the question put by Jesus. And the same question never ceases to be asked in one form or another, because in it and in the answer it provoked there lies the mystery which "reveals man to man himself", as the Council recalled (*Gaudium et spes*, n. 22).

That is why, alongside the replies to this question that was, is, and always will be crucial to Christianity, new formulations will always be put forward linking the "mystery of Christ"[2] with the "mystery of man" – with the most acute problems of man's existence. We need only recall the 1974 Synod of Bishops which dealt with evangelisation in the world of today. That too amounted to a great investigation on the theme of: "Who do people say the Son of man is?". Who is Jesus Christ for all the different continents of the world, for all the different societies, traditions, cultures, political situations? Jesus is the symbol of liberation from unjust structures both social and economic, but he is also the sign of liberation for people who are denied freedom of conscience and religious freedom, or who have those freedoms drastically curtailed at crucial points. He is in every way a reproach to affluent, acquisitive consumer societies. But he is the touchstone of identity for the African nations which are moving towards independence. He is a Word of divine wisdom for the ancient spiritual traditions and cultures of the East.

Here, in the Vatican, we are at the very centre of the Church, at the point where Peter's reply to the question: "Who is Jesus Christ?" is formulated. Let us first listen to what is said by individual men and women and by whole peoples. They all testify to the fact that in Jesus "the way, the truth and the life" are wide open, that great highway "along which – as the Council asserts – life and death are sanctified and take on fresh meaning" (*Gaudium et spes*, n. 22).

Notes

1. *Gaudium et spes*, n. 22.
2. Cf W. Kasper, *Jesus der Christus*, Mainz 1975.

XIII.

Meditation on the Glorious Mysteries

1. *The first mystery: the Resurrection*

"Haec est dies quam fecit Dominus" (Ps 118(117),24): This is the day the Lord has made. God had already made this day his own in his wonderful work of creation, which encompasses existence, good and glory. On that day God "rested" (Gen 2,2), and he commanded man to do likewise (cf Gen 2,3; Ex 20,8–11). Then, once death had entered the world through man's disobedience (cf Wis 2,24; Rom 5,12.17.19), God again made that day his own through his victory over death (cf Is 25,8; 1 Cor 15,54–55; Rev 21,4). He "is not God of the dead but of the living" (Mt 22,32). So this is the day made by God, the Creator and the Lord of life.

It is also a day on which "God made him both Lord and Christ" (Acts 2,36), this Jesus who was his "servant" (Acts 3,13). Jesus of Nazareth. He is the "servant of Yahweh" foretold by the prophet Isaiah (Is 42,1; 49,3.6; 50,10; 52,13) because in him all the prophecies were fulfilled (Lk 24,26–27; 1 Cor 15,3–4), especially the one concerned with humiliation, suffering and death (Acts 3,18). "We all like sheep were going astray, each going his own way, and in him the Lord struck at the sin of us all" (Is 53,6). When Jesus spoke of a temple: "Destroy this temple and in three days I shall make it rise again", his hearers did not know that "by 'this temple' he meant his own body" (Jn 2,19–21). It is he who taught us that man is God's temple and that God's Spirit dwells in him (cf 1 Cor 3,16; 6,19). The great servant of Yahweh allowed the temple of his body to be

destroyed, to be "emptied" to the point of death (cf
Phil 2,7–9), because he had faith in the day of the Lord, the
day when the Father in the power of the Spirit would rebuild
the temple of his body. In this way the Father would give
added radiance to the truth that he, Christ, is Lord of life
and death (Rom 14,9), Lord of human history into which
"death came" (Wis 2,24), Lord of creation.

"Look ... a spirit does not have flesh and bones as you see
that I have" (Lk 24,39), he said to his disciples, astounded to
see him enter that upper room where, "for fear of the Jews,
the doors were closed" (Jn 20,19). "Put your finger here and
see my hands. Bring your hand closer and place it in my
side" (Jn 20,27), said Jesus to Thomas who had said:
"Unless I place my hand in his side I will not believe"
(Jn 20,25). "Do not be sceptical, but believe!", said the risen
Lord. And Thomas made his profession of faith, saying: "My
Lord and my God" (Jn 20,28).

This is the day that the Lord has made! "Cor meum et
caro mea exultaverunt in Deum vivum" (Ps 84 (83),2).

2. *The second mystery: the Ascension*

"I came from the Father and I came into the world; now I
am leaving the world and returning to the Father"
(Jn 16,28). The Lord's words took effect forty days after the
Resurrection, when Jesus led the Apostles up the Mount of
Olives (Acts 1,3–12). Let us read those words again in the
context of all that the Master said to those who were with
him at the last supper (Jn 13–17). Let us read that
marvellous passage, in which Jesus speaks not only to the
disciples who were with him then but to all who will follow
him until the end of the world (Jn 17,20). In that farewell
discourse Jesus included all the most fundamental yet most
simple truths. An atmosphere of love, trust and openness to
both the Father and his disciples: that is what makes his
farewell, on the eve of his Passion and death, so appealing
for all time. "A little while and you will no longer see me;

again a little while and you will see me again ... . I am
going to the Father" (Jn 16,16–17). Philip had said: "Lord,
show us the Father". "Have I been with you so long, and yet
you do not know me, Philip? Anyone who has seen me has
seen the Father" (Jn 14,8–9).

That is how Jesus spoke in the upper room, when the
Apostles never expected to see him so humiliated, "emptied"
and crucified (Phil 2,7–8), never expected to see him risen
again, in his created body glorified already on earth. But
able to see him they certainly were, for forty days after the
Resurrection (Acts 1,3), until the day when he was "raised
up on high, and a cloud took him out of their sight"
(Acts 1,9). At that moment it was as if their seeing was at an
end, because he disappeared from their sight; but that seeing
nonetheless continued and still continues (cf Mt 28,20):
anyone who sees Jesus sees the Father too. The Church lives
thanks to this seeing bequeathed to her by the Lord. This
seeing is evident in the Gospel, and in prayer and sacrifice; it
permeates the Church's self-awareness and constitutes her
mission; it is the cause of her rejoicing in the midst of
troubles; it has become the foundation of her faith, hope and
love.

Heaven. ... During the last supper Jesus said to the
Apostles: "In my Father's house there are many dwelling-
places ... . I am going to prepare a place for you"
(Jn 14,2–3). And St Paul was to write: "Things that no eye
has seen, that no ear has heard, that no human heart has
understood, these things God has prepared for those who love
him" (1 Cor 2,9; cf Is 64,4; Jer 3,16).

3. *The third mystery: the descent of the Holy Spirit*

Jesus, who is "the image of the unseen God" (Col 1,15;
Heb 1,3), ascended to heaven. But a short while earlier he
promised his Apostles: "with the coming of the Holy Spirit
you will receive inner power to bear witness to me in
Jerusalem and Judea and Samaria and to the ends of the

earth" (Acts 1,8). The promise was at the same time a command. On their return from the Mount of Olives the Apostles persevered in prayer together, waiting for the great promise to be fulfilled (cf Acts 1,12–14). The Apostles at prayer in the upper room became an image of the Church then about to be born. With them was the Mother of Christ (Acts 1,14): the Church – as the mystical body of her Son, born of the cross (Jn 19,34) and the redemption (cf Pius XII, *Mystici Corporis*) – looked upon her from the beginning as a Mother, not only Mother of Christ but also Mother of the Church (cf Jn 19,26–27). Our Holy Father Pope Paul VI has expressed the same concept: Mary as Mother of the Church has her place in the "Credo of the People of God", in the Church's living faith (cf *Credo populi Dei*).

And now, on the day of Pentecost, the prayer of the Apostles and the Mother of Christ culminates in a great event which fulfils the risen Lord's promise (Acts 1,4). The external signs accompanying it are far less important than its inner meaning. Even though the sudden gust of wind, and the tongues of flame above their heads, and the extraordinary ability of these simple men to speak different languages are certainly not lacking in significance, what matters far more is that the Spirit of Jesus Christ, the Spirit of the Father and the Son, comes down to the upper room and, most important of all, enters the human spirit, enters the hearts of men. The Church came into the world simultaneously with that definitive change in the hearts of the Apostles. Only then did the Apostles whom Christ had chosen become his witnesses; only then did they start to testify to him before all Israel and before all who had come to Jerusalem to celebrate Pentecost. Their testimony is authentic, marked by "power from on high" (Acts 1,8; Jn 19,11); it is highly effective in that it bears fruit in the souls of those who listen. Thus the Church is born: the People of God of the new covenant.

The Church never ceases to fix her gaze on Christ. In him the Church sees the Father (Jn 14,9). And she never ceases to invoke the Holy Spirit: "Veni Pater pauperum, veni Dator munerum, veni Lumen cordium ..." (Sequence of the Mass of Pentecost).

4. *The fourth mystery: the Assumption*

The Mother of Christ, who follows her Son in leaving this earth, has a profound role within his mystery, the mystery of redemption of the world. This role colours the whole of her nature from the time of her Immaculate Conception until the end. The mystery of her Assumption is already present, though in embryo so to speak, at the time of her Immaculate Conception. The inheritance of death, the fruit of sin (Sir 25,24), did not affect the Mother of the Redeemer – thanks to the merits of her Son – and that was so from the moment of her Immaculate Conception (cf Pius IX, *Ineffabilis Deus*).

When we contemplate the last stages of Mary's earthly pilgrimage we gaze with adoration at all that flowed from that first grace bestowed on her – the grace to which the archangel testified: "Full of grace" (Lk 1,28). We embrace all that her grace has made possible when we celebrate the last "earthly" mystery of the Mother, which from the beginning has been called the "Assumption" (cf Pius XII, *Munificentissimus Deus*) just as the last earthly mystery of the Son has from the beginning been called the "Ascension".

In this mystery the hearts of the People of God are very close to the Mother of God, and this is especially true on the day of the Feast of the Assumption. Although in some countries – Poland for instance – this is no longer a major Feast, nonetheless the atmosphere is palpably that of a great Marian Solemnity. The People of God in my archdiocese celebrate the Assumption of Mary with great emotion. Many attend the so-called "obsequies" of Our Lady at the shrine of Kalwaria Zebrzydowska, a custom deriving from the tradition of the "falling-asleep" – *Dormitio* – of Our Lady.

Thousands of pilgrims attend the celebration of this "falling-asleep", which takes place on the evening before the Feast, at the so-called "sepulchre of Our Lady". Early in the morning on the day of the Feast, the procession makes its way to the main church. With great rejoicing everyone listens to the words of the liturgy: "Assumpta est Maria in coelum" and gives thanks to the Son for having welcomed in heaven the Mother who welcomed him on earth. The Church regards Mary's Assumption as a great sign of hope: "Then a great sign appeared in heaven: a woman clothed with the sun, with the moon under her feet and on her head a crown of twelve stars" (Rev 12,1).

5. *The fifth mystery: the Crowning of Our Lady*

> Hail, daughter of God the Father!
> Hail, mother of the divine Son!
> Hail, bride of the Holy Spirit!
> Hail, dwelling of the most Holy Trinity!

Those words are used by some believers when they recite the Holy Rosary. They are reminiscent of other words, those of St Paul in his first letter to the Corinthians: "Do you not know that you are God's temple, and that the Spirit of God dwells in you?" (3,16; 6,19): and they are even more reminiscent of words once spoken by Christ to his disciples: "If anyone loves me ... my Father will love him, and we shall come to him and dwell in him" (Jn 14,23). The Father came to dwell in Mary from the moment of her Immaculate Conception, and then in an even more perfect way at the time of the Annunciation, at the birth of her Son, on Mount Calvary, on the day of Pentecost, and finally at her Assumption. From the start she was "full of grace", and yet her grace was continually augmented. God dwelt in her more and more, and she became more and more a "temple of the Holy Spirit" (1 Cor 3,19; 6,19).

When she left this world, that temple ceased to be open to the things of this earth, of the visible world, and became open to the things of eternity, of the invisible and wholly divine world. This new openness brought her, above all, the vision of God (Jn 17,3). But at the same time it brought her a share in glory. Whereas here, on earth, our knowledge of God is only partial (1 Cor 13,9) – "Now we see only a blurred reflection" of him in creation – then we shall see him "face to face"; "now I know only in part – St Paul goes on — but then, just as I myself am known, I shall see" (1 Cor 13,12).

This seeing, this vision of God will confirm our love and also make it incomparably more potent. Vision and love: these await us at the end of our journey along the way of faith. In that everlasting vision the mystery of man, inextricably bound up with the mystery of the incarnate Word, will be revealed to the full. In that everlasting vision the mystery of the Virgin (cf Jn 19,26; Rev 12,1; Lk 11,27), whom the Father chose to be the Mother of his Son, will be revealed to the full. Her share in glory cannot be compared with that of any other created being (cf Jn 17,22). That is the wealth of meaning we must contemplate in the mystery of the Crowning of Our Lady in heaven.

XIV

The mystery of man: truth

1. *The truth and dignity of man*

"The fact is that only in the mystery of the incarnate Word is light shed on the mystery of man. ... Christ, who is the new Adam, by revealing the mystery of the Father and his love, also fully reveals man to man himself and makes his exalted vocation known to him" (*Gaudium et spes*, n.22).

From those words in the Pastoral Constitution on "The Church in the world of today" we can deduce the full meaning of the theme underlying this retreat of ours, the theme of "in Christ".

"In Christ", "in the mystery of the incarnate Word": the mystery of man is explained in the mystery of Christ, whose full historical dimension is attested by facts and events, by words, deeds and testimonies. All the essential problems of man find tangible expression in the Christ of history. The Incarnation and Redemption mean that Christ entered fully into all those problems, that he took upon himself the full weight of the burdens they impose, and that he gave them much deeper meaning, investing them with importance, nobility and purpose. The mystery of the Incarnation is a focal point in the whole plan of salvation, and its purpose is none other than the salvation of mankind. Salvation was not planned and effected independently of that which is essentially human; and that which is human has the divine stamp on it – it is an image of God (cf Gen 1,26). That is why for the divine work of salvation God drew on that which is human, essentially human and constitutive of man. If we approach the mystery of the Incarnation from this angle we can discern its profound significance as a focal point in the plan of salvation.

If the mystery of Christ – the historical Christ and the mystical Christ – "reveals the mystery of man to man himself", that is to say to mankind through the ages, then everything that is essentially human and constitutive of man is summed up in the mystery of Christ, and is expressed by Christ in either word or deed. Also relevant in this context is the teaching "de triplici munere Christi" – recalled by the Council – which assigns to the entire People of God a share in the threefold mission of the Messiah. A new and more profound picture of the Church emerges from this conciliar teaching: Christ is alive in the Church as prophet, priest and king thanks to the share in these functions enjoyed by the whole People of God (*Lumen gentium*, nn. 10–12; 31).

This idea in *Lumen gentium* has to be linked with the central theme of *Gaudium et spes* in which Christ is presented as a revealer of the full mystery of man and of human dignity. The Council stresses that man's essential dignity is inextricably bound up with Christ's message, his Gospel, which acts like leaven, either causing a stronger awareness of that dignity or else awakening a need to seek and attain it: "Whoever follows Christ, the perfect man, becomes himself more of a man" (*Gaudium et spes*, n.41).

So, we shall look first at Christ as prophet: "Christ, the great prophet who by the testimony of his life and the power of his words proclaimed the kingdom of the Father" (*Lumen gentium*, n.35). Then we shall at once turn to look at one aspect of man, because we are all the time looking to see how the mystery of man is revealed "in Christo".

Gaudium et spes has this to say: "Man is right to consider himself superior to the rest of the universe because of his intellect which makes him a sharer in the light of God's mind. By determined exercise of his talents through the ages he has certainly made progress in the empirical sciences, in technology and in the liberal disciplines. ... Our own age, more even than past centuries, needs wisdom if all man's new discoveries are to become more humane. The future of the world is in real danger unless wiser men are born and bred" (n.15).

The dignity proper to man, the dignity that is held out to him both as a gift and as something to be striven for, is inextricably bound up with truth. Truthful thinking and truthful living are the indispensable and essential components of that dignity. In a way the Council spoke even more profoundly on this subject in the Declaration *Dignitatis humanae* on religious freedom: "Because of their dignity all human beings, inasmuch as they are persons, have inherent in their nature a moral obligation to seek the truth, to adhere to the truth and to make the whole of their lives respond to truth's demands. They are in no position to meet that obligation unless they enjoy both psychological freedom and immunity from external coercion" (n.2).

2. Christ, a great prophet

Thus it is truth that makes man what he is. His relationship with truth is the deciding factor in his human nature and it constitutes his dignity as a person. At the same time that relationship with truth – an inner relationship, certainly, but one which also expresses itself externally – is an integral part of the "mystery of man"; this finds confirmation in Christ the prophet (Lk 7,16).

When Jesus was about thirty – the age prescribed by the Law for participation in public life – he went to the synagogue in Nazareth to read a passage from the prophet Isaiah. After reading it he said: "Today this scripture you have heard has been fulfilled ..." (Lk 4,20). We know that "his own people did not accept him" (Jn 1,11): they were unwilling to accept that the carpenter's son (Mt 13,55) was truly the one he claimed to be. That is how it is: "no prophet is well received in his own country" (Lk 4,24). He then left Nazareth and began to teach in towns and villages all over Galilee, bearing witness everywhere to the truth for the sake of which he had been sent by the Father (cf Jn 18,37). We know how the ordinary people welcomed and accepted him, and we know too that the witness he bore to the truth brought him in the end before two tribunals, first a Jewish and then a Roman one. And Pilate's tribunal was the setting for an encounter that brought into the full light of day the nobility of truth and the dignity of the man who bore witness to it. Pilate suspects Jesus of claiming sovereignty over Israel ("Are you the king of the Jews?"); when the imputation is denied he puts the question in a different form: "So you are a king?" Then Jesus replies: "It is you who say it, I am a king. For this I came into the world, to bear witness to the truth" (Jn 18,35–37). Even though Pilate the sceptic interrupts him to ask: "What is truth?", there is no doubt that truth emerged from that encounter as something real, constituting both Jesus's kingship and the dignity of man.

Christ, the great prophet is the one who proclaims divine truth; and he is also the one who shows the dignity of man to be bound up with truth: with truth honestly sought, earnestly pondered, joyfully accepted as the greatest treasure of the human spirit, witnessed to by word and deed in the sight of men.

Truth has a divine dimension; it belongs by nature to God himself; it is one with the divine Word. At the same time it constitutes an essential dimension of human knowledge and human existence, of science, wisdom and the human conscience. Every man is born into the world to bear witness to the truth according to his own particular vocation.

3. *Witness*

The words spoken during that encounter with Pilate ensure that Jesus the Christ is ever-present in the mystery of man. For man, truth is vital. True knowledge of himself, of the world, of God; truth in conscience, truth in knowing, truth in believing. Jesus said very clearly that the truth must not be denied to men or concealed from them (cf Mt 5,14–15) but must be openly professed (Mt 10,32). Truth has a social, a public dimension. Therefore man's right to the truth must never be denied. In our complex present-day world this denial can take different forms. One form it takes is that of "manipulation" of the truth – for instance the dissemination of some types of information and the suppression of others, the use of the mass media to pander to the cult of sensationalism typical of our times. Given these structures of present-day civilisation, given the pressures they exert, each and every man's personal responsibility inevitably becomes greater because the threat to the truth constantly becomes greater. People expert in the various fields have a particularly heavy responsibility, and here I am thinking especially of the responsibility to be exercised by Catholic theologians, writers and journalists.

Today man is being deprived of his right above all to the truth which affects his inmost being, the realm of his conscience and his relationship with God: this occurs when there is discrimination against this truth in its societal aspects. On this point we can learn a great deal from the conciliar Declaration *Dignitatis humanae*. What is at issue between the unjust civil power and the individual believer is not so much the faith itself – the truth cherished unseen in the heart of the believer – as the outward profession of that faith, the public witness to it. There is no lack of people determined at all costs to drive the divine truth underground into the catacombs, determined to deprive it of its public witness dimension, the dimension that is man's by right. There is real tragedy in situations which deny man the right to bear witness to the divine truth and at the same time force him to profess beliefs that fail to tally with – even flatly contradict – his own deepest convictions: man is thus forced to live a lie.

Past and present-day literature contains a number of highly disturbing descriptions of similar human alienation, by which I mean deprivation of that which constitutes man's human nature. And real life, both in individuals and societies, provides many examples of it. Regrettably no attention is paid to the Universal Declaration of Human Rights or to the various international agreements and conventions – or even to the state's own constitution. Reliance is placed on force alone: might is right. That is why our age stands in very special need of Christ, the one who said to Pilate: "For this I came into the world, to bear witness to the truth" (Jn 18,37); the one who in himself embraces, confirms and guarantees the essential profile of the "mystery of man" which is inseparable from man's relationship with the truth, his responsibility for the truth, his witness to the truth. Given our society today, in which falsity and hypocrisy reign supreme, public opinion is manipulated, consciences are bludgeoned, apostasy is sometimes imposed by force and there is organised persecution of the faith – sometimes camouflaged but all the more terrible for that – the Christ who bore witness to the truth is more than ever the Christ for us: "Christus propheta magnus" (Lk 7,16).

He is most certainly present with all disciples of his who want to share his prophetic mission, his responsibility for the truth both human and divine, his active witness. Yet he is also present with all men throughout the world, within a variety of political systems and in a variety of situations, who bear witness to the truth. Courageous witness of that kind is an effective counter to those who sow mistrust of one's fellow-men, and even to those who destroy not only man's sense of responsibility towards the truth but also his awareness of his absolute right to the truth. Let us therefore entreat Christ to continue always to send us the "spirit of truth" (Jn 14,17), the charism of truth, the strength to make the truth manifest to the complex and sometimes unruly world of today. Let us ask Christ to grant this to the whole of his Church.

4. "The sign of contradiction"

When the old man Simeon bent over the tiny child Jesus, he perceived in him "the divine light" (Lk 2,32) and the "sign of contradiction" (Lk 2,34). That "sign of contradiction" belongs in the deposit of divine truth. It was a basic component of the lives of the prophets (Mt 23,34). Some of them, like Jeremiah, did not find it easy to accept their mission; they even tried to find excuses for evading it:

> "You have seduced me, O Lord,
> and I have let myself be seduced;
> you used your strength against me and you con-
>   quered;
> I have become an object of constant derision;
> everybody makes a mock of me.
> For every time I speak
> I shout and cry aloud
> denouncing violence and oppression,
> so that the word of the Lord has become for me
> an object of insult and constant derision.
> I thought: I will not proclaim him,
> I will not speak in his name;
> but then in my heart I felt
> a kind of fire burning,
> shut inside my bones;
> I struggled to suppress it,
> but I could not.
> And I heard many slandering me:
> Terror on every side!
> Denounce him! We are determined to denounce him!
> All my friends awaited my downfall... .
> But the Lord was close beside me,
> like a mighty hero".

(Jer 20,7–11)

And so Jesus of Nazareth, like all who bear witness to the truth, became a sign of contradiction for those to whom he had been sent. The signs, the miracles he performed – the multiplication of loaves, the healings, the raisings of the dead to life – could not get the better of that fundamental contradiction which, humanly speaking, proved stronger than he was. Jesus sealed his witness with his own blood. And that is the inheritance he has bequeathed to the Church. The inheritance of salvific truth is an extremely demanding one, fraught with difficulties. Inevitably the Church's activities, and those of the Supreme Pontiff in particular, often become a "sign of contradiction". This too shows that her mission is that of Christ, who continues to be a sign of contradiction.

In recent years there has been a striking increase in contradiction, whether one thinks of the organised opposition mounted by the anti-Gospel lobby or of the opposition that springs up in apparently christian and "humanistic" circles linked with certain christian traditions. One has only to recall the contestation of the Encyclical *Humanae vitae*, or that provoked by the latest Declaration by the Sacred Congregation for the Doctrine of the Faith, *Personae humanae*. These examples are enough to bring home the fact that we are in the front line in a lively battle for the dignity of man.

The dignity of man, the dignity of the human person, has to be defended; but that dignity must not be made to consist in unbridled exercise of one's own freedom. And the freedom sought after by the campaigners in favour of abortion is a freedom at the service of pleasure unrestrained by norms of any kind.

All this strikes at the truth of the faith and of moral life, the truth which enables human dignity to be rightly understood. Man's dignity can be preserved only if human freedom is exercised justly and responsibly. It finds expression in the choices, such as marriage and priesthood, which affect one's whole life. It is the task of the Church, of the Holy See, of all pastors to fight on the side of man, often against men themselves! Christ fought like that, and he goes on fighting through the ages in men's hearts and in the human conscience. It is because of this that "the mystery" of every man is to be found in him. He is, in himself, the full and final measure of the mystery of mankind, so profound and yet so simple. All of us are servants of that mystery: the mystery of Christ, a great prophet!

"For a little longer the light is with you. Walk while you have the light, so that the darkness may not take you by surprise ..." (Jn 12,35). "If your eye is sound, your whole body will be bathed in light. But if your eye is defective, your whole person will be in darkness" (Mt 6,22–23).

XV.

The mystery of man: priesthood

---

1. *Priesthood in the teaching of Vatican II*

We are seeking to clarify "the mystery of man" in the light of "the mystery of Christ": Christ who "fully reveals man to man himself" as the Council teaches us (*Gaudium et spes*, n.22). Such an undertaking is a major contribution to that search for the truth about ourselves which, as we saw in our first meditation, is fundamental to all our reflection during a retreat. "Noverim me!"

In this present meditation we are going to concentrate on a subject that touches us very closely, our "own" subject so to speak. We are going to look at the "mystery of man" by way of the truth about the priesthood of Christ. Since each of us has his allotted share in that priesthood, such an approach seems particularly closely related to the lives we ourselves lead and the experiences that come our way.

Christ the Lord, high priest selected from among men (cf Heb 5,1–5), makes the new people "a kingdom and priests to his God and Father" (Rev 1,6; cf 5,9–10; *Lumen gentium*, n.10). Whilst making the essential distinction between the priesthood of all the faithful and the hierarchical priesthood, *Lumen gentium* goes on to explain how the whole People of God is endowed with a share in Christ's priesthood: "though they differ from one another in essence and not only in degree, they are nonetheless inter-related; for both, each in its own way, share the one priesthood of Christ" (n.10). When we meditate on how that one priesthood of the new and everlasting covenant is implanted in the souls of all the baptised, we attain to a deeper awareness of our own hierarchical priesthood; for it was within the dimensions of the common priesthood of all the faithful that our own was born, and then ripened to bear fruit and thus continually gain confidence and strength. We all remember how our own priestly vocation developed, that unique and unrepeatable journey that led each of us to the priesthood – be we priest, bishop or Pope.

"By regeneration and the anointing of the Holy Spirit, the baptised are consecrated to form a spiritual temple and a holy priesthood, so as to offer spiritual sacrifices through all that Christians should do, and to make known the wonders of him who called them out of darkness into his marvellous light (cf 1 Pet 2,4–10). Therefore all the disciples of Christ, persevering in prayer and praising God together (cf Acts 2, 42–47), offer themselves as a living sacrifice, holy and acceptable to God (cf Rom 12,1), everywhere bearing witness to Christ; giving, to all who ask for it, the reason for their hope of eternal life (cf 1 Pet 3,15)" (*Lumen gentium*, n.10). In that passage the Council makes it very clear that the "tria munera Christi" are closely related to one another and, consequently, that an equally close relationship exists between the shares in them enjoyed by each individual Christian and by the People of God as a whole.

This conciliar teaching seems to break down some barriers and correct some stereotypes to which many people have become accustomed. It shows priesthood to be one essential facet of the laity. The position adopted by the Council is evident in several different documents, for example in the fourth chapter of *Lumen gentium*, nn. 30–38, in the Decree on the Apostolate of the Laity, and so on. All the same – and this does need to be stressed – the tendency to "laicise" priests and religious is totally alien to the conciliar teaching. Such an interpretation can only be a distortion of that teaching and a fundamental error. Unfortunately in some instances that sort of error did occur. And an intervention by the Pope became necessary – and also in 1971 by the 3rd Synod of Bishops which dealt with the subject "de sacerdotio

ministeriali" – in order to declare those tendencies completely erroneous. The conciliar doctrine on the common
priesthood of all the faithful does not imply reducing
everything to the lay state, although it certainly does draw
attention to the enormous wealth of lay vocations within the
Church. Its true meaning is far nobler! In order to appreciate
it to the full we need to go back once again to the "mystery
of man" as it shows itself in the "mystery of the incarnate
Word", that is to say the mystery of Christ the priest. Christ
brought with him into the world the essentials and the
fulness of priesthood: "You have prepared a body for me:
neither burnt offerings nor sin offerings were pleasing to you.
Then I said: See, I come to do your will, O God"
(Heb 10,5–7). It was on that basis that Jesus accomplished
his sacrifice and instituted the Eucharist, and still makes the
whole people "a kingdom and priests for God" (Rev 1,6).

Priesthood understood in that sense goes right back to the
existential interrogative concerning man. "What is man?
What is the meaning of pain, evil and death, which continue
to exist despite all progress? What is the real worth of all
these victories achieved at such great cost? What does man
bring to society and what can he expect from it? What is to
come after this present life?" (*Gaudium et spes*, n.10).

The Council asks those questions at the end of an analysis
of the situation in the world of today, questions which it said
were of prime importance. And here is the Council's
diagnosis of the present situation which led on to the
questions: "The truth is that the imbalance from which the
present-day world suffers has links with the graver imbalance
inherent in the heart of man. For within man himself many
elements conflict with one another. On the one hand he
experiences in a number of ways his limitations as a created
being, while on the other hand he is aware of being boundless
in his aspirations and of being called to a higher life.
Charmed by many different attractive possibilities, he is
always obliged to choose some and reject others. Further-
more, being weak and sinful, he often does what he would

rather not do and fails to do what he would prefer to do"
(*Gaudium et spes*, n.10).

2. *Priesthood as a reply*

What is priesthood, be it the common priesthood of all the
faithful implanted in the soul of every Christian by baptism
or the hierarchical priesthood? Of its very nature priesthood
is a reply to the insistent, profound, fundamental questions
asked by man, by the whole "human family", about the
meaning of the created world, the meaning of the whole of
reality in which man belongs existentially and yet which he
surpasses. The priest, simply by being who he is, expresses
this meaning and at the same time conveys it to the world
and to man in the world. He expresses it because in him all
reality is embraced. He conveys it not by elaborating a set of
arbitrary ideas but by embracing the truth, as truth's
"prophet and servant".

I often talk to our seminarists. Every year I try to meet a
few of them if only for a short while. And very often I ask
them how and when they became aware of their vocations
and of their desire to enter the seminary and become priests.
The answers vary enormously: one said that he had thought
of nothing else ever since he became an altar-boy; another
said that after passing his school exams he had come to
Cracow intending to study law at the university, and really
didn't know himself how he came to end up in the seminary;
but he was quite certain that he was now on the right track.
The answers I get testify above all to the action of grace on
young souls, but they also show the wonderful processes of
human thought – still youthful but already mature – about
God and man and the world. Priesthood is an expression of
the meaning given to man and the world by their relationship
with God. And the profoundest of truths about man and the
world is that they both belong to God, Creator and
Redeemer. This truth leads to understanding of the "sacrificium laudis" (Ps 50 (49),14) natural to the created world

and entrusted to man in order that man may become a living expresssion of the glory of God (cf Ps 116(115),17; Heb 13,15) – the "sacrificium laudis" which expresses the homage paid to its Lord by the whole of creation (cf Ps 66(65),4) and which enables man to become the spokesman so to speak for the created world (cf Rom 8,19–21). And all this matures in souls that are still young. It does so, of course, against the background of the common priesthood of the faithful. Its foundation is the one constructed in these souls by the sacraments of Baptism, Confirmation and the Eucharist – by the Eucharist above all. Not to mention the sacrament of Matrimony in a good christian family, and the "sacrament of the Church" in a good parish.

Priesthood reaches to the depths of the whole existential truth of the created world, and above all the truth of man. A song which is a favourite with young people in Poland says a great deal: "When I gaze at the starry sky on a clear, calm, quiet night, and wonder if life has any meaning, I turn to you, our Father, O God my Lord. Do not remember that at times I have gone wrong. You know that I am always yours, and that I want to go your way only". The human mind's stamp of priesthood as truth gives definitive meaning to the priest's own life and to the lives of all men, the meaning which that song conveys by the words: "You know that I am always yours, and that I want to go your way only". Those words also express awareness of man's freedom. It is a freedom which allows us to make choices, especially in all that affects the basic orientation of our lives.

Let us listen again to what Vatican II has to say about this: "True freedom ... is to the highest degree a sign of the divine image in man. God willed to leave man 'in the hands of his own counsel', so that he might spontaneously seek his creator and attain freely, through adherence to him, to full and blessed perfection. Hence man's dignity requires him to act in accordance with conscious and free choices, to be motivated and guided by his personal convictions and not by blind impulse or external pressure" (*Gaudium et spes*, n.17).

3. *The hermeneutics of the mystery of man*

The human will – or rather the human heart – impels man to be "for others", to have generous relationships with others. It is in this that the essential structure of personal and human existence consists. Man exists not merely 'in the world', not merely 'in himself'; he exists 'in relationship', 'in self-giving'. Only through disinterested giving of himself can man attain to full discovery of himself. More than anything else the priesthood, linked with celibacy by Gospel precepts and centuries-old tradition, gives expression to this truth about man. The priesthood in particular is the form of self-expression of the man for whom the world's ultimate meaning can be found only in the dimension of the transcendental: in turning towards God who, as the fulness of personal Being, in himself transcends the world. Without relationship and without self-giving, the whole of human existence on earth loses its meaning. "What is the real worth of all these victories achieved at such great cost? ... What is there to come after this present life?" (*Gaudium et spes*, n.10), asks the Pastoral Constitution. Surely every thinking man asks the same questions. If this ultimate relationship, this prospect for man "beyond this world" is lacking, then all the achievements of civilisation, all the progress made in culture, science and technology will lead only to man's ruin.

Christ's priesthood flowed from the paschal mystery. Our priesthood is not ours but his. We must therefore draw the most profound truth about life from Christ's death and resurrection. "May he make us an everlasting gift pleasing to you" (3rd eucharistic prayer): that is how we speak to the Creator, our Father, in the name of Christ and in "in persona Christi", and at the same time in the name of every creature. Because of its own meaning the priesthood will always contain within itself a profound "hermeneutics" of the mystery of the world and above all of the "mystery of man". Any world which sought to delete the priesthood from its structures would deny its own self, and above all would destroy human nature in its most essential aspect. Are there perhaps some moves in that direction in the world of today? Most certainly there are! We can detect them even in this ancient christian continent of Europe. Everybody is well aware that here, in the very centre of the christianised world, the scaffolding has been erected for the "new world" programmed as a world "without God". In some countries this programme has been imposed on men by force. There, confronted by the doctrinaire materialism that holds sway, we can see disappearing all the signs and symbols of that wonderful hermeneutics of the world, in particular the secret of man and man's transcendence, brought by Christianity and even by other religions. Either they are disappearing altogether or else they are being strictly limited. New towns are being built, districts full of high-rise housing into which thousands of people are crammed. But no churches are being built; in fact church-building is not allowed. A church would spoil the beautiful picture of the "new world" dreamed of as a "world without God". Man with his inner truth, his hunger for the transcendent, is left stranded; he is only marginal, not even that, to the "march of civilisation", the building of modern society.

That is the course being taken by the "brave new world" described by various doctrinaire thinkers and visionaries, for whom priesthood is the direct opposite of their own concepts. When Christ is denied all rights of citizenship, those same rights are denied to men; and when the "death of God" is proclaimed, the "death of man" is being planned as well. That is the way things are going in many parts of the world, and it all started long before today. Pioneers of pastoral work among French workers – Père Godin and Père Michonneau for instance – have drawn attention to the fact that the building of whole new districts without a single church was already used during the Third Republic as a method of de-christianisation. Today that same method is in use in many countries. Man is bound to move in that direction unless awareness of sharing in the priesthood of Christ by virtue of baptism is aroused in each Christian, each community, each district. But when that does happen, those men and women – not mainly we priests and bishops but the laity themselves – will go and tackle the authorities and demand, with all the firmness at their command, that their new district be provided with a church. They will demand a church in the name of their rights as citizens; but above all they will demand one in the name of that fundamental truth about the world and mankind which is contained in Christ, in priesthood, in the human temple of God. Without a church no district in that "new world" will ever discover its own true meaning; nor will it ever be fully "human".

4. *Prayer*

The priest is a man of prayer: "vir orationis". At this point we need to spend more time on the fundamental subject of priestly prayer: liturgical prayer – the Eucharist, the sacraments, the breviary – and non-liturgical, private prayer, especially the interior prayer of thought, of heart and will, of adoration and contemplation, of silence and recollection. Perhaps I may venture a short summing-up of the whole question of prayer in the life of the priest. Priesthood is both prayer of existence and human vocation: inherent in it are both the unceasing prayer of the whole world, "sacrificium laudis" (Ps 50(49),14), and the prayer of the man of flesh and blood, the consecrated "homo Dei" who at the most important moment of each day lends his voice to Christ himself so that the words of consecration may be uttered.

The priest is, in himself, the living expression of the prayer of the whole created world. This is the truth declared by St Paul in his letter to the Romans: "We know that until now the whole of creation has been groaning and suffering birth-pangs; not only the created world but we ourselves, who possess the first fruits of the spirit, groan inwardly as we await our adoption, the ransoming of our bodies. For in hope we have been saved" (Rom 8,22–24).

Precisely. Prayer is an act of hope. It is an expression of hope, the sign of hope for the world, for mankind. Prayer enables us, as the Apostle says, to look towards the fulfilment of our hope, towards that reality to which the human heart aspires: "If we still hope for that which we do not see, patience assists us to wait for it" (Rom 8,25).

Yes, indeed. Prayer is indispensable for persevering in pursuit of the good, indispensable for overcoming the trials life brings to man owing to his weakness. Prayer is strength for the weak and weakness for the strong! Here is what the Apostle has to say: "Thus the Spirit too comes to help us in our weakness, because we do not know how to ask for the right things; but the spirit himself intercedes for us, with sighs that words cannot express" (Rom 8,26). Prayer can be said to be a constitutive element of human existence in the world. Human existence is "being directed towards God". At the same time it is "being within the dimensions of God", a humble but courageous entering into the depths of God's thought, the depths of his mystery and his plans. It is a kind of drawing on the source of divine power: will and grace. It is also, as St Paul says, the work of the Holy Spirit in us; "the Spirit himself intercedes for us, with sighs that words cannot express". And the Spirit, says the Apostle in another letter, "the Spirit sees into all things, even the depths of God" (1 Cor 2,10).

Priesthood is the supreme prayer of all things: of man and of the world.

XVI.

The mystery of man: conscience

1. *Munus regale*

"The fact is that only in the mystery of the incarnate Word is light shed on the mystery of man. ... Christ, who is the new Adam, by revealing the mystery of the Father and his love, also reveals man to man himself and makes his exalted vocation known to him" (*Gaudium et spes*, n.22). Let us look once again at those words from Vatican II which are the main inspiration for our meditations about mankind. The Council here expresses a deeply held conviction shared by us all: that man cannot be understood without Christ and that it is impossible to educate him, to develop his human nature and his vocation in life without Christ.

As we continue our meditation on how the whole question of man can be traced back to the Church's teaching on the threefold mission of Christ *(tria munera Christi)*, it is now time for us to consider the *munus regale* (cf *Lumen gentium*, n.31). The conciliar teaching concerning this kingly function seems remarkably akin to present-day man's thinking and feeling, and this in a sphere where it might have been expected to give rise to at least "verbal" difficulties. For especially in our democratic societies – democratic in name if not always in fact – people now fight shy of categories such as "king" and "kingdom" or, rather, "reign". But the problem of power as such has in no way ceased to be relevant to our time: on the contrary, it constantly engages people's attention, arousing strong emotions as well as stimulating careful thought.

The fact that the teaching "de munere regali Christi" was

expounded in the chapter "De laicis" in *Lumen gentium* is worth remarking. Let us read an extract from it: "Christ, having made himself obedient unto death and being therefore exalted by the Father (cf Phil 2,8–9), entered into the glory of his kingdom. To him all things are made subject until he subjects himself and all created things to the Father in order that God may be all in all (1 Cor 15,27–28). Christ has communicated this power to his disciples, so that they too may be established in royal freedom, and so that by self-abnegation and a holy life they may not only overcome the reign of sin in themselves (cf Rom 6,12) but also, by serving Christ in others, may humbly and patiently lead their brethren to the King, serving whom is reigning" (n.36).

This exposition goes to the heart of the problem. Here we have the meaning attributed by Christ to his "kingdom". "Munus regale" is not the right to exercise dominion over others; it is a manifestation of the "kingly character" of man. This kingly character is embedded within the structure of the human personality. Still referring to the laity, *Lumen gentium* goes on: "The faithful must therefore get to know the inner nature of the whole of creation, its value and its due contribution to the glory of God. ... Therefore by their competence in secular fields, and by their activity inwardly supported by the grace of Christ, let them perform their own tasks effectively, so that all the good things created in accordance with the plan of the Creator and in the light of his Word may be developed thanks to human effort, technical skill and civic culture for the benefit of all men without exception, and may be more fittingly distributed among them, and may make their own contribution to universal progress in human and christian freedom. Thus Christ, through the members of his Church, will ever-increasingly illumine the whole of human society with his saving light" (n.36).

It is a superb text! It certainly deserves to be read and interpreted in the light of contemporary anthropology, social ethics and economics. Any analysis of it must take account of the whole philosophical tradition, beginning with Aristotle (where "praxis" is complementary to and consequent on "theory") and proceeding all the way to present-day philosophy, marxist especially, which puts "praxis" before "theory" and deduces all its explanation of reality – especially the reality of man – from that "praxis", that is to say from the work by which man "created himself" within nature. The limited time at our disposal does not permit us to do all that now, during our meditation.

It is a fact, however, that Vatican II sees in human "praxis" a manifestation of the "kingly character" of man, of his dominion over the earth, nature and the world. Two terms that belong in the biblical and gospel vocabulary have to be stressed: "dominion" (cf Gen 1,26; 1,28; Ps 8,6; Wis 6,3, etc) and "kingliness" (cf Ex 19,6; Rom 5,17; 2 Tim 2,12; 1 Pet 2,9, etc). These two terms belong to christian dialectic, to anthropology, to ethics, which at this point differs essentially from dialectical materialism. Underlying the truth about man professed by the Church "usque ad sanguinem" lies the deep conviction that man cannot be "reduced" to matter alone. If he has mastery over matter, he has it solely thanks to the "spiritual element" (cf Rom 8,23) which is inherent in him and which expresses itself in his knowledge and his freedom, that is to say in his activity. So one could acknowledge that a partial truth is contained in the assertion that "work creates man". Yes, it does create; but it does so precisely because it is a work – an activity, a "praxis" – of man: "actus personae".

2. Conscience

The conciliar teaching on the "kingliness" of man goes deeper still. All human work, and all that it produces in any field of endeavour, shapes the human personality; but it does so not because of the objective value of what it produces but because of its own moral worth – a distinctively human and personal element in all man's activity, man's "praxis".

The Church's magisterium gladly acknowledges that human work is of decisive importance both to the economy and to social life. In this context, natural law principles as they affect private property have been made clear in two Encyclicals – John XXIII's *Mater et Magistra* and Paul VI's *Populorum progressio*. All the same, an exclusively "economic" approach to understanding the truth about work is decidedly "anti-humanistic". Work is not the only thing that "produces" man; if we wish to remain faithful to a correct analysis of the human person, we must assert very clearly that self-fulfilment, or self-creation, has its source in man's moral conscience, his spiritual centre. Let us read what *Gaudium et spes* has to say on the subject: "In the depths of his conscience man discovers a law he has not made for himself but which he must obey, a law which always calls on him to love and do good and shun evil, and which when necessary speaks clearly to his heart and says: do this; shun that. The fact is that man has within his heart a law written by God; man's dignity lies in obedience to it, and he will be judged accordingly. Conscience is the most secret core and sanctuary of man, where he finds himself alone with God, whose voice can be heard in his inmost being. ... The more an upright conscience prevails the more persons and social groups move away from blind caprice and seek to conform to the objective norms of morality. Often conscience errs through invincible ignorance without thereby losing its dignity. But this cannot be said of any man who makes little or no effort to seek what is true and good, or of a conscience that becomes almost blinded as a result of sin that is habitual" (n.16).

That synthesis is brief but highly accurate. The dignity of the human person has its foundation in the conscience, in that inner obedience to the objective principle which enables human "praxis" to distinguish between good and evil. The conscience warns against evil and urges man towards good. It wants man to become firmly attached to what is good, not just for the time being but more profoundly: it wants him to become, in the words of St Thomas, "bonus in quantum homo"; it wants him not to lose that underlying good which is his human nature itself. Man's obedience to his conscience is the key to his moral grandeur and the basis of his "kingliness", his "dominion"; and this – ethically speaking – is also a dominion over himself. Obedience to conscience is a key element in the Christian's share "in munere regali Christi". Obedience to conscience, which in its turn is obedient to the divine law of love, is what equates "serving Christ in others" with "reigning" (cf *Lumen gentium*, n.36).

3. *The sacrament of Penance*

There we see the full extent of the truth about the Christian's share in "munere regali", in the "kingliness" of Christ himself.

The subject of conscience is bound to arise in the course of a retreat; indeed all retreats are built around it. It explains one particular aspect of the "mystery of man", the mystery that is "fully revealed in the mystery of the incarnate Word" (*Gaudium et spes*, n.22). Jesus Christ always pointed out the close connection between his own mission and the mystery of the human conscience. John the Baptist, foretelling the imminent coming of the Messiah, had said: *"Metanoeite!"* – "Repent!" Jesus, before healing the paralytic, said to him: "My son, your sins are forgiven you", and then: "Stand up and walk" (Mk 2,5.11). Jesus made it very clear that the bodily healing merely confirmed the fact that he had power to forgive sins, power over the human soul. "Which is easier? To say to the paralytic 'Your sins are forgiven you' or to say 'Stand up, pick up your stretcher and walk'?" (Mk 2,9). He said that in reply to the objections being raised by some of the onlookers: "Why does this man say such things? He is blaspheming. Who but God alone can forgive sins?" (Mk 2,7).

Jesus forgives sins by the power of his cross (cf Col 2,14; 1 Pet 2,4) and resurrection (cf Rom 4,25; 2 Cor 5,15). The first time he entered the upper room after the resurrection he spoke the words which convey the principal benefit conferred by the paschal mystery: "Receive the Holy Spirit; to any whose sins you forgive, those sins will be forgiven" (Jn 20,22–23). Jesus does not levy accusations against the sinner; he is the sinner's redeemer, the shepherd who gives his life for his sheep. Sin is beyond all doubt central to his teaching, to his concern for man. His attitude when faced with sin, or rather with sinful man, shows that he always has a keen appreciation of the dignity – one might say the "kingliness" – of the man who, having accepted the truth about his sinfulness, thereupon repents.

This same "kingly" aspect of man can be perceived in the whole practice of the sacrament of Penance. When a man goes down on his knees in the confessional because he has sinned, at that very moment he adds to his own dignity as a man. No matter how heavily his sins weigh on his conscience, no matter how seriously they have diminished his dignity, the very act of truthful confession, the act of turning again to God, is a manifestation of the special dignity of man, his spiritual grandeur. We know how dependent this grandeur is on God's grace. Confessors like St John Vianney could say a great deal on this subject. There is real grandeur in that moment of inner truth about oneself when one turns directly to God: "Tibi soli peccavi, tibi soli... ." says the Psalmist (Ps 51(50),4). "Father, I have sinned against God and against you" says the prodigal son. In that moment of inner truth about himself man puts himself in touch with God in a very special way. This is the grace bestowed by the sacrament of Penance, the grace that flows from the crucified Christ. It is he who accomplishes it, in him it all comes about; in him, crucified and risen again, these wonderful meetings between God and man take place, meetings which – even though they take place in the relative dimness of faith – nonetheless have in them something of the nature of a meeting "face to face" (1 Cor 13,12). The potency of grace is apparent in both the depth and the simplicity of this meeting, qualities which are owed on the one hand to one's realisation of a truth about oneself and on the other hand to one's deep certainty of being able to put one's trust in God, certainty that he can and will forgive. "Who but God alone can forgive sins?" (Mk 2,7).

In recent years both theology and pastoral considerations have stressed the ecclesial aspect of the sacrament of Penance. Sin causes great damage to society, the Church and humanity. This aspect was heavily stressed in the early centuries. Indeed it never has been ignored, even though the practice of private confession could convey an impression of individualism in this matter. Undoubtedly the sacrament of Penance is to the good of the individual person within the community of the Church. But one must not allow that to diminish the grandeur of the personal meeting between man and God in the inner truth of conscience: "Tibi soli peccavi...". In this sacrament there is always utter simplicity in the relationship between the "Father who sees in secret" (Mt 6,6) and listens in secret and the man in the inner truth of his conscience, the man experiencing a moment of the "kingliness" bestowed on him by Christ in order that he may be "established in royal freedom" and "by self-abnegation and a holy life overcome the reign of sin in himself" (cf *Lumen gentium*, n.36).

4. *Munus pastorale*

Christ's kingship cannot be fully understood without that moment of victory over sin which is the work both of grace and of man's free will. Every confessor must go down on his knees, so to speak, before the secrets of grace and the human conscience. Even though the confessor certainly is judge, counsellor and teacher to one of his brothers or sisters, he must exercise those attributes and functions with the greatest possible respect for the "mystery of man" which is explained in the "mystery of Christ". It is Christ crucified and risen again who is present in the confessional, just as by means of the priest he is present by the altar during celebration of the Eucharist, at the sickbed to which the priest brings the oils of anointing, and in all the Church's sacramental ministrations.

"Munus regale": the kingly mission of Jesus Christ is handed on to the Church in a very special way in the pastoral authority exercised by the bishops under the direction of the successor of Peter, and by priests and deacons under the direction of the bishops (cf *Lumen gentium*, nn.28–29). The source of pastoral authority – as well as its justification, its example and its ideal – is Christ the good shepherd shown us by the Gospel. This is the basis of the truth that all spiritual authority in the Church must be directed towards developing and making evident the dignity of man, his "kingliness" which comes to him from Christ the good shepherd. "I know my sheep and my sheep know me" (Jn 10,14). "I give my life for my sheep" (Jn 10,15). "And when he finds it he takes it on his shoulder, rejoicing" (Lk 15,5). And so on. The history of the Church through the ages is full of examples of excellent followers of the good shepherd.

As we come to the end of this meditation let me conjure up one picture that means a great deal to bishops and pastors. It is that of the bishop making the canonical visitation of a parish. That parish is not simply a part of his Church in the administrative sense; it is the community of the People of God which, in spite of all man's weaknesses, sins and vices, possesses both the triple mission of Christ and the seal of "kingliness" bestowed by him. One has to know how to detect and appreciate that "kingliness", that dignity, in a variety of circumstances: in children being confirmed, in married couples renewing their sacramental promise in the presence of their bishop, in the sick and the old whom one visits at home or in hospital. The dignity of man, his "kingliness", come from Christ, who makes the whole People of God "a kingdom and priests" (Rev 1,6): this is apparent in the joy that surrounds the bishop's stay in the parish.

The more difficult man's life becomes – family life, the

life of society, the life of the world – the more need there is for the figure of the good shepherd who "gives his life for his sheep" (Jn 10,11) to stand out clearly in man's awareness. The bishop who visits the communities of his Church is the authentic pilgrim who arrives at one after another of the good shepherd's sanctuaries preserved by the People of God, sharers in the kingly priesthood of Christ. Indeed, such a sanctuary is to be found in every man; for every man's "mystery" can be explained and resolved only in the "mystery of the incarnate Word" (*Gaudium et spes*, n.22).

XVII.

The prayer in Gethsemane

---

1. *Sharing the prayer of Jesus*

In this meditation we are going to return to a subject already spoken of: prayer. But this time, rather than *talking about* prayer, I would like us – as far as is humanly possible, and with the aid of grace – to *share in the prayer of Christ himself.*

We know how often he used to pray completely alone, withdrawing from the company of his disciples and keeping himself totally free to converse with the Father. More often than not he did this while the others were resting: "And he spent the whole night in prayer" – "pernoctans in oratione Dei" (Lk 6,12), as we read in the Gospel. On one occasion only did Jesus specifically ask the Apostles to share his prayer with him, and that was in Gethsemane where the Master had gone, together with them, on Holy Thursday night. All that Jesus had said and done in the course of the last supper was still fresh in their minds and hearts. And then, leaving most of them behind on entering Gethsemane, he took just three of them with him: Peter, James and John, the ones he had taken to Mount Tabor, and said to them: "Stay here and keep vigil with me". And then, moving a short distance away from them, he prostrated himself and prayed (cf Mt 26,38–39). It was all a clear appeal to them to share his prayer.

Why at that specific moment? Why on that occasion only? Perhaps because he had already made them sharers in his mystery in one way: he had given them bread to eat saying: "This is my body offered in sacrifice for you"

(Lk 22,19), and wine to drink saying: "This cup is the new covenant in my blood shed for you", charging them to "Do this in remembrance of me" (Lk 22,19–20). In so doing he had made them sharers in his mystery at its most profound level.

2. *Great understanding of mankind*

Jesus begins to pray. Moving a short distance away from the three, he begins to converse with the Father – as on so many other occasions. This time, however, his prayer is decisive: it originates in the depths of his soul and discloses the whole truth of his human nature, not only showing his acute anxiety at this particular moment in his life as Son of man but also bringing together, so to speak, all the anxieties felt by the one who said of himself: "I am the good shepherd. The good shepherd gives his own life for his sheep" (Jn 10,11). Jesus embarks on this prayer with an immeasurable universal concern for each and every one: "I know my sheep and my sheep know me" (Jn 10,14). This prayer reflects Jesus's great knowledge and understanding of man and the whole of human nature, sunk in the abyss after the first sin and subsequently straying further and further from the will of the Father, with consequences more frightening than those of the original disobedience.

This prayer is the prayer of great understanding of mankind, for it was uttered by the one of whom scripture says: "He had no need of any man's testimony concerning another, for he knew very well himself what was in each one" (Jn 2,25).

3. *"Father, if it be possible, let this cup pass me by"*

What are the words he uses in this prayer? We know them very well: they are few but unforgettable, simple but highly charged with the emotion of the hour – the hour in which the servant of Yahweh must fulfil the prophecy of Isaiah by saying his 'Yes'. "Jesus Christ was not 'Yes' and 'No'; in him there was only 'Yes' " (2 Cor 1,19).

Christ's words in Gethsemane are very simple, wholly appropriate for expressing the most profound of truths and the most important of choices. Jesus says: "Father, if it be possible, let this cup pass me by; nevertheless, not my will but yours be done" (Mt 26,39). We may remark that by this time it was no longer possible for the cup to pass him by, because it had already been passed on by him to the Church and had become "the cup of the new and everlasting covenant", the cup of the blood "which will be shed" (Mk 14,24). And yet, in spite of all that, Jesus says: "If it be possible, let it pass me by ...".

What is the meaning of: "If it be possible"? Is this not the prayer of the Son of God who, in all the truth of his human nature, "sees into all things, even the depths of God" (1 Cor 2,10) in the Holy Spirit? Since he shares to the full the mystery of God's freedom, he knows that events do not necessarily have to take this course; but at the same time he shares God's love, and so he knows that there is no other way. He had in fact come to Gethsemane in order to receive the death sentence that had long ago been pronounced, in eternity no doubt (Col 2,14). So, having come, he fell on his knees and prayed – as if that death sentence, already pronounced in eternity, had to be pronounced there, at that very hour. "If it be possible, may this cup pass me by ...".

Prayer is always a wonderful reduction of eternity to the dimension of a moment in time, a reduction of the eternal wisdom to the dimension of human knowledge, feeling and understanding, a reduction of the eternal Love to the dimension of the human heart, which at times is incapable of absorbing its riches and seems to break.

The sweat which appeared like drops of blood on the face of Jesus as he prayed in Gethsemane is a sign of the acute torment he suffered in his human heart. "And Christ, in the days of his flesh, offered prayers and supplications to him who could save him from death ..." (Heb 5,7).

4. *A meeting between the human will and the will of God*

This prayer is in fact a meeting between the human will of
Jesus Christ and the eternal will of God, which at this
moment can be seen as the will of the Father concerning his
Son. The Son had become man in order that this meeting
might express all the truth of the human will and the human
heart, anxious to escape the evil and the suffering, the
condemnation and the scourging, the crown of thorns, the
cross and death. He had become man in order that this truth
might then serve to reveal all the grandeur of the love that
expresses itself in a "gift of oneself", in sacrifice: "God loved
the world so much that he sacrificed his only-begotten Son"
(Jn 3,16). In this hour that "eternal Love" has to give proof
of itself by the sacrifice of a human heart. And it does indeed
give proof of itself! The Son does not shrink from giving his
own heart, for it to become an altar, a place of complete
self-abnegation even before the cross was to serve that
purpose.

The human will, the will of the man, meets the will of
God. The human will speaks by means of the heart and
expresses the human truth: "If it be possible, may this cup
pass me by". But at the same time the human will surrenders
itself to the will of God, as if passing beyond the human
truth, beyond the cry of the heart: it is as if it were taking
unto itself not only the eternal judgment of the Father and
the Son in the Holy Spirit, but also the power that flows
from God, from the will of God, from the God who is Love
(1 Jn 4,8).

All prayer is a meeting between the human will and the
will of God; for this we are indebted to the Son's obedience
to the Father: "Your will be done". And obedience does not
mean only renunciation of one's own will; it means opening
one's spiritual eyes and ears to the Love which is God
himself, God who loved the world so much that for its sake
he sacrificed his only-begotten Son. "Here is the man". After
his prayer in Gethsemane Jesus Christ, Son of God, rises to

his feet fortified: fortified by the obedience which has enabled him once again to attain to Love, as gift from the Father for the world and for all mankind. He rises to his feet and goes back to his disciples saying: "Look, my betrayer is close at hand" (Mk 14,42).

5. *The mystery of Redemption*

This is the third time he has broken off from prayer and gone back to them. And, just as before, he finds them asleep. He had reproached them already: "Could you not keep vigil with me for one hour? Stay awake and pray so as not to give way to temptation: the spirit is willing but the flesh is weak" (Mt 26,40–41). But even that warning had not kept them awake. Peter, James and John did not know how to respond to his call to prayer addressed to them as they entered Gethsemane. The words Jesus now speaks for the second and third time become a reproach, a reproach of concern to every disciple of Christ. In one way the Church still hears those same words: the reproach addressed to the three Apostles is accepted by the Church as if it were addressed to herself, and she tries to fill the gap left by that lost hour when Jesus remained completely alone in Gethsemane. The Apostles did not know how to respond to the appeal to share the prayer of the Redeemer, and they left him completely alone. This showed that the mystery of redemption required the Son to remain alone in intimate converse with the Father. This total solitude creates a dimension fully appropriate to the divine mystery, which at the same time is a human activity on the part of the Son of man.

And now the Church still seeks to recover that hour in Gethsemane – the hour lost by Peter, James and John – so as to compensate for the Master's lack of companionship which increased his soul's suffering. It is impossible to reconstruct that hour in all its historical veracity: it belongs in the past and remains for ever in the eternity of God himself. Yet the desire to recover it has become a real need for many hearts, especially for those who live as fully as they can the mystery of the divine heart. The Lord Jesus allows us to meet him in that hour – which on the human plane is long since past beyond recall – and, just as he did then, invites us to share the prayer of his heart: "Cogitationes cordis eius in generationem et generationem, ut eruat a morte animas eorum et alat eos in fame" (Entrance antiphon, Mass of the Sacred Heart of Jesus). And when "from generation to generation" we enter into the designs of his heart, from that sharing there flows the mystical unity of the Body of Christ.

How rich in meaning that "Stay awake!" now becomes: "Stay awake, so as not to give way to temptation!" Christ hands over to us that hour of great trial, which always has been an hour of trial for his disciples and his Church.

"I am the vine ..." says the Lord, and these words are most appropriate to the situation in Gethsemane. "I am the vine and you are the branches ... As the branch cannot of itself bear fruit unless it remains joined to the vine, so also not one of you, unless you remain in me..." (Jn 15,5). "I am the true vine, and my Father is the vine-dresser. Every branch in me that bears no fruit he cuts right out: and those which do bear fruit he prunes, so that they may bear more fruit still" (Jn 15,1–2).

The prayer of Gethsemane goes on to this day. Faced with all the trials that man and the Church have to undergo, there is a constant need to return to Gethsemane and undertake that sharing in the prayer of Christ our Lord. That prayer – according to the standards of human reckoning – remains unanswered. But at the same time, in virtue of the principle: "My thoughts are not your thoughts and my ways are not your ways" (Is 55,8), it marks the beginning of the great victory, the beginning of the redemptive work on which man and the world still draw and always will draw, because the Redemption makes manifest the nature and extent of God's love for mankind and for the world (cf Jn 3,16).

And so the prayer of Gethsemane is not left unanswered.

XVIII.

Mysterium mortis

---

1. *Eschatology and "sacrum"*

Jam fines saeculorum ad nos devenerunt – "The end of the ages has come upon us" (1 Cor 10,11).

In the Constitution on the Church, the second Vatican Council devoted a whole chapter to eschatology (*Lumen gentium*, nn. 48–51). There is more to this subject than is covered by our traditional tracts *De novissimis* on the eschatology of mankind: the Council speaks of "the eschatological nature of the pilgrim Church and her union with the heavenly Church". So this eschatology of the Church is *sui generis*. In it we find themes and emphases that are absent from the traditional eschatology of mankind.

In the old manuals and in the catechisms, the treatment given *De novissimis* was largely confined to the following truths: death, judgment, heaven, hell and purgatory; but the conciliar eschatology of the Church and the world is dominated by the truth of the "making-new" of all things in Christ (cf Eph 1,10), of the new heaven and the new earth (cf Is 65,17; Rev 21,1) anticipated in a way in the paschal mystery of Jesus Christ (cf 1 Cor 5,7). This truth concerning the nature of the Church prepares the world for the "making-new" already begun in Christ (cf Col 3,10; Rev 21, 2–5). Thanks to the incarnation of the eternal Word, the world and humanity have inherent in them the seeds of the fulness of time (cf Eph 1,10). Here is the Council's eschatology in its essentials:

"The final phase of time has already come upon us (cf 1 Cor 10,11), for the making-new of the world has been irrevocably decreed and in a real way is anticipated in this present world" (*Lumen gentium*, n.48).

"Christ, when he was lifted up from the earth, drew all men to himself" (cf Jn 12,32).

"The Church, to which all are called in Christ Jesus and in which by God's grace we attain to sanctity, will achieve fulfilment only in the glory of heaven, when the time will come for the restoration of all things" (*Lumen gentium*, n.48).

These splendid truths, which seem to spring from the heart of the New Testament and especially from the Apostles' letters, do not merely stress the truth that the Church is on pilgrimage; they also present the meaning and purpose of this pilgrimage. The truth of this pilgrimage, which likens the earthly life of man to the road he travels towards his final destination, is deeply rooted in the human consciousness (for example Ps 16(15),11; 119(118),26–32; Lk 24,32–35; Jn 14,5–6). Because men are persons, with intellect and freedom setting them apart from all other creatures in the visible world, they cannot see their own lives in any other light. The pilgrimage analogy, the comparison with the road to be travelled, is particularly apt for mankind (cf Heb 13,14). *Homo viator*. A pilgrim on his way to the absolute (cf *Lumen gentium*, nn. 49–50). These and similar expressions bear out the eschatological character of the human being in the religious sense too. Man reaches out towards God, his final destination. He travels towards the holy city (cf Ps 122(121),1–4; Is 2,2–5; 35,10), the sanctuary, which is accessible to him alone. The dimension of the "sacrum", the "sacral" values: these constitute the highest and most definitive sphere of human life and the sphere of man's most complete self-fulfilment. In this dimension man becomes more fully himself. Through the medium of the "sacrum" the whole of human life is sublimated, raised to "above"; its natural tendency to remain "below" is thus countered (cf Jn 3,3–7; 8,23; Col 3,1–2, Jas 1,17; 3,15.17). By contemplating the sacral values and adopting them as his own, man progresses in self-affirmation and self-fulfilment.

All the research which has shown the sacral dimension to meet a basic need of human nature contradicts the philosophical and scientific negations contained in systems of thought which see the "sacrum", especially the supreme "Sacrum", as the source of man's alienation, his "dehumanisation" in some sense. This sometimes results in a frenzied determination to desacralise, to fight against whatever is "sacred", against every "sacrum" at every level of human life, particularly in social and public life. The firm intention is to force man to live totally apart from any "sacrum" whatsoever, so as to make him "man" and nothing more – that is to say "desacralised".

But all the experience of the Church and of humanity goes to show that the "sacrum" is of decisive importance for the full humanisation of man. In this field the Church has vast experience accumulated over the centuries: one has only to think of all the beatifications and canonisations of the Servants of God, of the whole history of human sanctity through the centuries and generations. In itself this rich history, running its course uninterrupted, lends real support to the Council's eschatology of the Church, which describes the pilgrim Church as united with the Church of the saints in heaven (cf Eph 5,26–27; Rev 5,10; 7,9–10; 19,7–8).

2. *"Progress" or "trial"?*

This conciliar eschatology of the Church, which is full of trust in the final victory of good over evil (Jn 16,33; Rom 8,37; 1 Jn 5,4; 2,13–14; Rev 4,5; 5,9–10; 7,14–17; 12,10–11, etc) and in the promised "making-new" already begun in Christ, coincides very closely with human experience. From the very beginning the Church has been concerned with eschatology. But the Church is also in contact with all the real dimensions of history, which is now reaching out for development and progress, and is also bound up with the crisis in morals and authentic human culture.

The word "progress" is on everyone's lips and in everyone's thoughts; but real life confronts us with so much loss, calamity and ruin that one wonders whether, broadly speaking, regress is not triumphing over progress. *Gaudium et spes* seeks to give the right criterion for evaluating man's progress when it says: "A man's worth lies more in what he *is* than in what he *possesses*" (n.35): but is this the criterion by which progress is being evaluated today?

The course of history – in our own day especially, perhaps – shows an ever-greater contrast between man's enormous material gains and his moral shortcomings, his falling-short in the sphere of what he is. One can quite safely say that in the sphere of what he is man fails to match what he possesses.

The diagnoses and prescriptions of dialectical materialism, and all the secular "eschatology" of temporality, are being attacked in a number of studies and reports – for example the one by the Club of Rome on "the limits of development" – which forecast, using purely scientific methods, that present-day civilisation will be engulfed in a catastrophe caused by excessive exploitation of natural resources, destruction and pollution of the natural environment, and demographic problems – not to mention the head-spinning expenditure on armaments. The writers of these reports demand – in the final analysis – that the discrepancy between what man possesses and what he is be wiped out. All the same one cannot see man – even taken globally – having the strength to do that.

If we open the scriptures we find in all these books a wealth of facts to confirm this sad truth about the world and man (cf Gen 3,5–6; 18,20; Deut 32,15–21; Judg 2,11–13; Wis 14,22–29, etc). We find the same truth in St Paul's letter to the Romans: "And since they declined to consider knowing God, God left them open to perverse ways of thinking, so that they commit acts that run counter to every law, full as they are of all kinds of iniquity, perversion, cupidity and malice. Libellers, slanderers, haters of God, arrogant, boastful braggarts, devisers of evil, rebellious to their parents, lacking good sense, honesty, affection, pity" (Rom 1,28–31). Clearly this is a picture of ancient Rome, one we are familiar with from other descriptions such as the one in *Quo Vadis* by Sienkiewicz. But doesn't it bear some resemblance to the picture our own times present? Much has been written describing the present state of mankind, about the environment and about society, from the standpoint of the so-called "three worlds" into which humanity is divided. The picture of human life under the totalitarian regimes is a terrible one; for there man is deprived of his essential raison d'être, his freedom of decision and action. There is no lack of literature bearing sad witness to our "century of progress" which has become the age of a new enslavement, the age of the concentration camp and the oven. Even under the liberal regimes, where men have grown sick from too much prosperity and too much freedom, human life presents a saddening picture of all kinds of abuses and frustrating situations. Isn't this borne out by the phenomena of drug-addiction, terrorism and kidnappings of innocent people?

Added to all that there is an ever-widening gap between the prosperous societies and the Third World, where millions endure hunger and live in conditions of dire poverty (cf *Populorum progressio*).

Gaudium et spes tells us that: "The whole of human history is pervaded by a fearsome battle against the powers of darkness, a battle that started when the world began and that will go on, as the Lord says (cf Mt 24,13; 13,24–30 and 36–43), until the last day. Embroiled in this conflict, man constantly has to struggle in order to maintain his link with the good; and he can attain his own inner unity only at the cost of great effort and with the help of God's grace" (n.37).

Thus the concepts of "progress" and "development" relate not only to man's existence in the world but also to his way of life, and above all to "hard work", "struggle" and "trial".

One has the impression that the advances made by the world fashioned by men bring with them an increase in man's burdens, making being a man – with responsibility for good and evil – more testing that ever (cf Gen 4,6–7; 1 Kings 3,9; Ps 1; Ps 119(118), etc). And throughout the world centres of tension grow more numerous. This is what we have come to at the end of this second millennium after Christ. Is there not an analogy with what Jesus said about the destruction of Jerusalem and the signs that would presage his second coming? "Take care that nobody leads you astray. Because many will come in my name and say: I am the Christ! and they will lead many astray. Then you will hear of wars and rumours of wars. See to it that you are not alarmed, because all this has necessarily to take place; but it is not yet the end. Nation will rise up against nation, and kingdom against kingdom; there will be plagues, famines and earthquakes in various places. But all these things will be only the beginning of the sufferings" (Mt 24,4–8). And it is highly significant that with all this in view Jesus predicted that his disciples would be persecuted: "Then they will torture you and kill you, and you will be hated by all nations because of my name. Then many will take offence and betray one another and hate one another. Many false prophets will arise and will lead many people astray. And because of the great increase in wickedness many people's charity will grow cold. But he who perseveres to the end will be saved" (Mt 24,9–13).

3. *Mysterium mortis*

"We do not know the time when the earth and humanity will come to an end, and we do not know the way in which the universe will be transformed" (*Gaudium et spes*, n.39). But one thing is clear to all of us: our death. "That men die once is certain" (Heb 9,27). The inevitability of death is known to all alike. *Gaudium et spes* tells us: "In the face of death the enigma of human existence reaches its peak. Man is distressed not only by the thought of pain and the progressive deterioration of his body but also, and even more, by the fear of an end to himself once and for all. But his heart's instinct guides him aright when he abhors and rejects the idea of any total destruction and final annihilation of his person. The seed of eternity inherent in man, who cannot be reduced to mere matter, rebels against death. All the endeavours of technology, however useful they may be, fail to calm man's anxieties: no prolongation of the biological lifespan can satisfy that desire for further life which is unconquerably present in his heart". (n.18).

This "fear of an end to himself once and for all" is perhaps *ex contrario* the principal argument in favour of the value of life, of existence, by virtue of the fact that "being is good",[1] that "being is better than non-being".[2] Here we have the most profound and essential affirmations of philosophy based to some extent on the experience of death. Present-day philosophy, especially existentialism, shows great interest in this problem. But man does not in fact experience death, which of itself is a "terminal situation" beyond the actual experience of anybody; men only register the fact of death, although they can experience the reality of dying. Although many do experience that, each man finally dies alone.

Perhaps the loneliness of dying is best expressed in Christ's words from the cross, words which have often given rise to much thought on the part of theologians and other writers: "My God, my God, why have you forsaken me?" (Mk 15,34; Mt 27,46; cf Ps 22(21),1). Perhaps the Son of God, true man, wished to express in those words the human reality of death, the human experience of dying. Even though the soul of Christ never lacked clear vision of God, this experience remained nonetheless real. Perhaps his experience of human dying was even more acute precisely because of his vision of God, in the same way as his shouldering the burden of man's sin in Gethsemane.

The eschatology of the world remains – as we have heard – a great mystery. Thus in this world, which in the form in which we know it is passing away (1 Cor 7,31), each and every man enters the "terminal situation" of death, approaches the end of his days on earth, gives up his spirit. According to world statistics, thousands die every hour. And each one "rejects the idea of any total destruction and final annihilation of his person. The seed of eternity inherent in man, who cannot be reduced to mere matter, rebels against death". But in this same reality, in this dimension of every dying person – be he centenarian or two-day-old infant – there remains present the promise, the "guarantee of our inheritance" (Eph 1,14; cf Eph 1,18; Heb 9,15) given to us in Christ, and in some way "mysteriously contained" in the new life which, in human and world history, began with Christ. "Hence the final phase of time has already come upon us, for the making-new of the world has been irrevocably decreed and in a real way is anticipated in this present world" (*Lumen gentium*, n.48). And this "making-new", this new life, takes place in man (cf Rom 6,4; 2 Cor 5,17; Eph 2,15; Col 3,10, etc). Every man.

So every dying man has in him the biological reality of death, the "dissolution of the body", and also the human experience of dying, in which "the seed of eternity ... rebels against death", and this seed "is inherent in every man, who cannot be reduced to mere matter"; finally every man has inherent in him the mystery of a new life which Christ has brought and which he has grafted on to humanity.

Every human death without exception has this dimension, even if the dying man, or those around him, may not be conscious of this reality. For it is due not to man's consciousness but to God's plan and revelation. As all men are sanctified "in Christ Jesus" (cf 1 Cor 1,2.4) their death means a prolongation of this life "in Christ": "For if we live, we live for the Lord; if we die we die for the Lord. So whether we live or whether we die we belong to the Lord" (Rom 14,8)." 'So long as we are in the body we are exiled far from the Lord' (2 Cor 5,6) and having the first fruits of the Spirit we groan inwardly (cf Rom 8,23) and long to be with Christ (cf Phil 1,23)" (*Lumen gentium*, n.48).

This describes the human, and in particular the christian, life – a life of awareness of the mystery of Christ. Any life lived in such awareness is in a way ratified in death: "Cupio dissolvi et esse cum Christo" (cf Phil 1,23) – that is to say I desire a dimension of life that has been begun in me by Christ. The Christian is aware that he anticipates this; and that awareness is the distinguishing mark of his dying.

Present-day personalistic philosophy seeks to emphasise this personal sense of death and dying.[3] Even though a man does not choose his own death, nonetheless by choosing his own way of life he does, in a way, choose his own death too. Thus his death becomes the perfect ratification of his life and of the choice he has made. The Apostle's words just quoted – and also the passage from *Lumen gentium* – coincide with this personalistic view of death. "That same charity spurs us on to live more fervently for him who died for us and rose again (cf 2 Cor 5,15). And so we strive to be in every way pleasing to the Lord (cf 2 Cor 5,9); and we put on God's armour so as to be able to stand firm against the assaults of the devil and put up a strong resistance on the evil day (cf Eph 6,11–13). Since we know neither the day nor the hour, we need to be constantly on our guard, as the Lord has warned us" (*Lumen gentium*, n.48).

Notes

1. Sum. Theol. I, q.5, a.3.
2. Sum. Theol. I, q.4, a.1 ad 3.
3. K. Rahner, *Zur Theologie des Todes*, Herder 1958[4]; J. J. Landsberg, Essay on the experience of death, Warsaw 1967.

XIX.

The way of purification

1. The mystery of sin

"Amplius munda me" (Ps 51(50),4).

The mystery of sin is very closely bound up with the mystery of death (cf 2 Thess 2,7). "The ultimate explanation of both the sublime vocation and the profound distress experienced by men is to be found at one and the same time in the light of divine revelation" (*Gaudium et spes*, n.13). And so man turns to revelation in order to understand the reality of sin and its connection with death. The connection is made clear in the book of Genesis by the two trees: the tree of life and the tree of the knowledge of good and evil. Between them these two symbols convey the greatest and most timeless truth about human existence. "You may eat freely from every tree in the garden, except that you must not eat from the tree of the knowledge of good and evil; for if you do eat of it you will assuredly die" (Gen 2,16–17). Here we have evidence that the mystery of death and the mystery of sin are inseparable from one another (cf 2 Thess 2,7). Vatican II's teaching on man and his vocation describes the nature of sin as follows: "What we know from divine revelation is in accord with experience. When man scrutinises himself he becomes aware both that he himself is capable of evil and that he is surrounded by many kinds of evil that cannot come from the good Creator. By frequently refusing to acknowledge God as his beginning, man destroys the relationship he ought to have with his ultimate end, and in consequence introduces disorder into his attitude to himself, to others and to all created things. Thus man finds himself divided within himself. Because of this, all human life, whether individual or collective, has the characteristics of a dramatic struggle between good and evil, light and darkness" (*Gaudium et spes*, n.13).

As we have already seen, man's sin is less all-embracing than that of Satan. Satan's sin is total and wilful denial on the part of a created being; it is outright refusal of God as Father and Love, as source and end of fulfilment: "amor sui usque ad contemptum Dei". St Thomas teaches that sin of this gravity presupposes another level of perfection in that same being, a level of intellect and will different from that of man.[1] Man's sin has not and cannot have that gravity. Human sin consists in turning away from God, principally because of disorder in man's attitude to created things. This is well brought out by the passage just quoted from *Gaudium et spes* which speaks of sin destroying man's "proper order" "in his attitude to himself, to others and to created things" (n.13). Nonetheless, even in this form human sin is freely-willed "opposition" to God on man's part; thus it is an "abuse of freedom" and a desire to "pursue one's own ends independently of God" which arises out of man's frequent refusal "to acknowledge God as his beginning". Moreover we know that sin varies in intensity (cf, for example, 1 Cor 3,12–15; 1 Jn 5,16). Both scripture and tradition make this distinction. Scripture speaks of sins that result in exclusion from the kingdom of God (cf 1 Cor 6,9; Jas 5, 19–20).

Is it possible for man – in his life, his activity, his intention – to know when that moment has arrived, the moment known as mortal sin? If we have in mind the vital breaking of the link with the divine "tree of life" which is grace, that obviously cannot be known because it is part of the mystery. Nevertheless this mystery is inherent in man, and it is a mystery that is by no means unconnected with his subjectivity, his consciousness and his will. Hence he has his own criteria of fault and sin, criteria which enable him to live, in the light of faith, the mystery of death caused by sin, and to seek the new birth brought to us by Christ (cf Rom 6,3–14), the forgiveness in the Holy Spirit which Christ entrusted to the Apostles (cf Jn 20,22–23). However we also know that sin at its worst is a reality that not only affects a man's subjective conscience and will but also affects his relationship with God the Holy Spirit, the fount of grace. In fact Christ said explicitly that every sin committed by man can be forgiven in this life or in the life to come, except that there will never be any forgiveness for sin against the Holy Spirit (cf Mk 3,28–29). These words demonstrate clearly that remission or non-remission of sin is dictated not by considerations of moral evil – a purely human dimension – but by consideration of the relationship with the fount of grace, the Holy Spirit. If that relationship were to be destroyed, even indirectly – and present-day theology seems to lay particular stress on this point – the sin would never be remitted (cf Mt 12,32).

Man is capable of committing the sin against the Holy Spirit, the sin that is analogous – by human standards – to the sin of Satan; but in man's case the sin has not and cannot have the same inner gravity. In spite of everything it is, and always will be, sin on a scale proportionate to man, proportionate first of all – it would seem – to the complex network of conditioning factors affecting human life. The sin of Satan contains a dimension of absolute, conscious and freely-willed denial of God, a choice meant to be irrevocable and constantly reiterated. It is this that results in the state of rejection known as hell (Mt 22,13; 25,26–30.41.46; Jn 5,29). Which human sin enters the dimension of that rejection and leads to it, and when, is part of the mystery. Obviously all this has a place in the eschatological perspective of the faith (*Lumen gentium*, n.48).

2. *The law of purification*

As is apparent even from a summary analysis, sin in all its theological reality, its effect on man's relationship with God, is inescapably a fact of human life; and it causes man to fall short in his treatment of himself, of others and of the world. The whole of this "temporal" dimension of sin, linked with creation and with time, is reflected in the wonderful revealed teaching about man's purification from sin – purification that is effected by "temporal punishment". The concept of punishment calls for clarification.

Although punishment in itself causes suffering, humiliation, deprivation of freedom – things which grievously wound a man – it nevertheless serves a good purpose (or at least it should) in that it restores justice and good order and helps to rehabilitate the offender, leads to his purification. We all know from present-day experience how the whole system of crime and punishment can lead to abuses, how "the good of society" is made the excuse for judging and condemning men not for any wrongdoing but for their disagreement with the tenets of the system, or often simply because they are misfits. We have all heard about terrible indictments – sometimes followed later by rehabilitation – and sentences inflicted on people disgracefully liquidated in the name, so it is said, of law and order. Nonetheless, these abuses cannot change the basic truth about punishment. Unjust application of judicial systems on the part of men only underlines the need for ultimate justice, the justice of God himself.

God's justice embraces not only the inevitability of punishment for crime (so admirably portrayed in ancient Greek tragedy) but also the law of purification of sinful man, who is called in Christ Jesus to a destiny in eternity. This law of purification has roots deep in human existence, and it points the way for rigorous thought about the life of man and of society. When we 20th century Poles reflect on our past, on what our 19th century parents and grandparents must have thought at the time of the partition of Poland, our thoughts turn not only to the so-called political errors which are a matter of history but above all to the sins, our own moral crimes. "The fathers have eaten sour grapes and the children's teeth are set on edge" (Jer 31,29; Ez 18,2). The work of reparation and reconstruction began with an "examination of the national conscience", as in every confession. And now too, when one looks at the fate of our continent after the second World War, similar thoughts and conclusions emerge. It seems to me impossible to understand fully what is often called the "crisis of the Church" in Europe unless one delves into the various periods of history and strips off the incrustations formed by sin (social inequalities, colonialism, imperialism); perhaps we also need to apply, up to a point, the analogy of the human sub-conscious, the bad conscience, as several present-day thinkers do in the field of anthropology and ethics[2].

All the same, within the divine order of justice – which makes itself felt in world events through the heart of every man – neither description nor psychological analysis of the subconscious is of prime importance; what matters most of all is the law of purification, which reveals both the temporal and the eternal perspectives of mankind. The inner structure of the human personality shows how deeply rooted this law is within man. One need only consider – in the light of one's own experience as well as in the light thrown back by the great mirror of literature – the purifying function performed by the human conscience. Shakespeare spoke of it:

> Give me another horse! Bind up my wounds.
> Have mercy, Jesu! Soft! I did but dream.
> O coward conscience, how dost thou afflict me!
> ...
> My conscience hath a thousand several tongues,
> And every tongue brings in a several tale,
> And every tale condemns me for a villain.[3]

It is well known that our conscience not only decides

whether our actions are good or bad but also approves or disapproves of us. When it disapproves it chastises and torments us with its pangs of remorse. And this is the fundamental temporal punishment within the purifying function willed by God. Our pangs of conscience are a form of suffering that purifies. They are more far-reaching in their inward effect than any other temporal chastisement; for not only does a man really experience within himself the malice of sin, crime, injustice, injury, but he is also able to set himself free from it again – an inner liberation but nonetheless a real one.

Inner purification, rightly called moral, comes by way of suffering; but the purifying process is not mechanical. It is well known that suffering does not always pave the way to good. Sometimes it seems to open the door to further evils: for example, poverty leads to thieving and prostitution. The creative aspect of suffering, linked as it is with man's moral purification, remains a mystery. One's reflection on this mystery can start from the experience of all sorts of people, including the saints. St Ignatius of Loyola's conversion took place on a bed of pain. Hospital chaplains could testify to a number of similar conversions occurring during a period of suffering and brought about by suffering. It seems as if during suffering man is better able to appreciate the fundamental meaning of values which generally escape his notice; he seems to be more conscious of the fragility of his existence and therefore of the mystery of his creation, of his responsibility for his life, of his sense of good and evil and, finally, of the inexpressible majesty of God. In holy scripture we find magnificent books about human suffering; and many verses in them, especially those attributed to the just man Job, could put new life into our meditation.

When "the hand of the Lord struck" (cf Job 19,21) the chosen people, it seemed like total calamity. The last of the davidic kings had been imprisoned, the country had been devastated, the priests and all the educated classes had been deported to Mesopotamia; above all, Israel's glory and hope, the holy city and the temple of Zion, guarantee of Yahweh's presence and protection, had fallen. "God has delivered me into the hands of evildoers and put me at the mercy of the godless" is Job's lament (16,11), and in terrifying phrases he curses the day he was born (3,1–9). Even the most faithful in Israel are assailed by doubts: Why? Why does God destroy his own work? "How long is the oppressor to go on insulting your name, O God, and how long is the enemy to go on reviling you? Remember, Lord: the enemy is insulting you; a godless people is reviling your name" (Ps 74 (73),10.18). "O God, why do you reject us for ever, why does your anger blaze against the sheep of your pasture?" (Ps 74 (73),1).

And God replies. His reply, the word of God that "makes the earth fertile and never returns without making it yield fruit" (cf Is 55,10–11), is the beginning of the new stage in the history of salvation. Salvation is born of suffering that is apparently meaningless. It was in his suffering that Job found the Lord.

3. *The mystery of purgatory*

Part of the law of suffering – a law which is, however, less inflexible than that of death – is that it entails loneliness for man. This loneliness is not always evident, nor does it occur at every level of suffering. The limits of human endurance are not reached in every illness; but the closer the suffering gets to those limits, the more the sufferer has to endure it alone. That loneliness can be seen in the story of the just man Job. And when loneliness becomes the occasion for man to meet God, the purifying dimension of suffering is seen to extend beyond the confines of this life. Jesus Christ introduces every man into the purifying dimension of suffering which goes beyond the confines of this life. "The Lord himself came to set man free and strengthen him, making him inwardly new and casting out 'the prince of this world' (Jn 12,31) who kept him a slave to sin (Jn 8,34). For sin

diminishes man, hindering his progress towards fulfilment"
(*Gaudium et spes*, n.13).

It is here, on this road leading to man's fulfilment, to his
final perfecting in Christ, that we find the mystery of
purgatory.

"While some of the disciples of Christ are pilgrims on
earth, others who have passed from this life are being
purified" (*Lumen gentium*, n.49). The revealed doctrine on
purgatory gives formal expression to this law of purification
which the most holy Lord must have engraved deep within
his covenant with mankind. The mystery of purgatory has to
be discerned in relation to the supreme holiness of God which
man has to approach more closely in his final perfecting
through Christ. One explanation of this mystery makes use
of the concept of a debt of "temporal punishment" that has
to be discharged after life on earth. This explanation is
convincing enough from an objective point of view. But in
purification man remains the subject.

The law of purification and the reality of purgatory
certainly have a profound objective meaning from which
their subjective meaning stems. Both arise out of the need for
man to be spiritually prepared for union with the living God
in charity. In one sense this union expresses the degree of
purity attainable by the created human spirit. Here,
obviously, we are presupposing a whole order of grace,
because union with the living God far exceeds the dimensions
and the entitlement by right of any created being. God
himself wills this union. It is he who leads man towards it in
Christ and in the Holy Spirit, so it is he who determines the
degree of perfection required for this union. Therefore the
mystery of purgatory is explained not only by the order of
justice and the need for expiation through temporal punishment but also – and perhaps primarily – by the order of
charity and union with God.

Man needs this mystery for his interior life, for his ascesis,
for his steady approach towards the living God in the

darkness of faith; although the darkness hides the face of the living God it unveils the infinite majesty of his holiness.

Perhaps the inner experience of the mystics comes closest to this truth. St John of the Cross wrote: "With such punishment God greatly humbles the soul in order greatly to uplift it later; if God did not arrange for these feelings, once experienced, to subside quickly, the soul would die within a few days.... These feelings are sometimes so intense that the soul seems to perceive hell and its own perdition wide open to its gaze. These souls are numbered among those who descend live into hell (Ps 55,15), for they endure in this life the purgatory due to be endured in the next. And so the soul may pass through this state, or it may not, or it may remain in it only a short time; for one hour of it in this life is of more avail than many in the next".

And so the magnificent text in which the Council expounded the eschatological nature of the Church was bound to include all this "way of purification" which takes various forms during man's earthly pilgrimage and then in purgatory. Attachment to the world, attraction to sin, conversion to God, turning away from sin, purification from attachment during the dark night of the senses, the dark night of the spirit, preparation for the great meeting "face to face": "Cor meum et caro mea exultaverunt in Deum vivum". "My heart and my flesh rejoice in the living God" (Ps 84(83),3). And this, even in the darkness of faith, is the sole fount of our hope and our strength.

"Amplius lava me ab iniquitate mea et a peccato meo munda me". "Wash me thoroughly from my iniquity and cleanse me from my sin" (Ps 51(50),2).

Notes

1. Cf Sum Theol. I, q. 62, a. 8, ad 2; I, q. 64, a. 2.
2. Cf, for example, P. Ricoeur, *Husserl et le sens de l'histoire*, Revue de Métaphysique et de Morale, 1949.
3. *Richard III*, Act V, scene 3, 177–8, 193–5.

XX.

The glory of God is man alive[1]

1. *The mystery of the final consummation*

"Jam ergo fines saeculorum ad nos devenerunt" (cf 1 Cor 10,11). The second Vatican Council turns again to these words of the Apostle to the gentiles in its treatment of the eschatological nature of the Church. Because the ultimate reality, *to escaton*, is part of the mystery of the Church it has a place in the Constitution on the Church (n.48).

If we are to appreciate fully all that is said in chapter VII of *Lumen gentium*, we need to set that chapter alongside chapter I, in which the Church is viewed within the mystery of the most Holy Trinity. "And then came the Son, sent by the Father, who chose us in him before the foundation of the world and predestined us for adoption as sons, because he willed to bring all things together in him (cf Eph 1,4–5.10)" (n.3).

The Son, co-eternal and consubstantial with the Father, who entered the history of man and the world, and in whose name the Holy Spirit was sent to "dwell in the Church and in the hearts of the faithful as in a temple (cf 1 Cor 3,16; 6,19)" (n.4), embraces in the supreme mystery of God, the most holy mystery of God, the entire human reality of the Church and, through the Church, the entire dynamism of "the world".

This "communio personarum" (n.24) deep within the godhead, deep within the Word and the Gift, has taken into its embrace both humanity and the world. "In him we live and move and have our being" (Acts 17,28). That is why the description "People of God" applies more aptly to the Church than to the Israel of the Old Testament. The moment of incarnation of the Word, the eternal Son, through the working of the Holy Spirit marked the introduction of a completely new dimension of God's presence in humanity and the world. A totally new relationship was established between temporality and eternity, between what is historical and what is eschatological. Because of this the New Testament presents us with a clearer and more profound picture of the definitive consummation (cf Col 1,19–20; Eph 1,3–14).

The Old Testament did not envisage so full a meeting between God and man and the world, a meeting which sets both man and the world on the road to God, on the road to the final consummation.

There is a need to re-think the so-called "novissimi" in the light of this final consummation. Perhaps the tradition we have grown up in has linked judgment, heaven and hell too closely with anthropology and ethics. It has been customary to start from man – who tends towards complete happiness but can never achieve it in the world, in temporality – and from moral consciousness – for which temporality is "not enough" because in this world man does not find complete justice. All the same, an understanding of eschatology from man's angle alone, taking into account only man's desires and aspirations (Kantian teaching comes to mind here), is insufficient as a basis for proper understanding of the so-called "last things". The right basis, as the Council has so admirably pointed out, is the plan of salvation revealed by God; and that plan, according to the logic of revelation, is that of the consummation of all things in Christ.

"He is the image of the unseen God, the first-born of all creation, because in him all things in heaven and earth were created, visible and invisible ... all was created in him and for him. It was the Father's good pleasure to make all fulness reside in him, and through him – who re-established peace by shedding his blood on the cross – to reconcile to himself all that exists on earth and in heaven" (Col 1,15–16; 19–20).

Thus the consummation, which is fundamental to all eschatology, flows from the trinitarian mystery, which the cross of Christ enlarged to take on the additional dimensions of man and the world. The cross of Christ begins the "missio Spiritus Sancti", the mission of the Spirit who is the "spirit of life": "through him the Father restores life to men, dead through sin, until one day he will bring their mortal bodies to life in Christ (cf Rom 8,10–11)" (n.4) and lead the Church into the fulness of truth (cf Jn 16,13). The blood of Christ's cross marks the beginning of all that mysterious and essentially divine work of salvation, justification and sanctification which is already shaping in outline the final consummation that is to come.

In spite of all the many types of resistance offered by men, and in spite of all the successes registered by the various opponents of the Gospel, all human affairs are interwoven with strands of this divine activity, the economy of grace and salvation. And even though, to our eyes, it seems as if the very opposite of the future consummation is on the way, even if human affairs in some places look more like the work of the apocalyptic Beast (cf Rev 13–14), nonetheless God's action – redemption, justification, sanctification – does penetrate through all these manifestations of the evil accumulated throughout history, and consequently does almost inevitably make all things tend towards final consummation in Christ.

God's action in no way restricts man's freedom; it leaves man free to try out his own plans and his own solutions; it even allows evil to exist, in order to bring out the good that is latent in all human initiatives. At the same time this action of God in the world, this divine economy (cf 1 Tim 2,4) in human affairs, does lead – through all the complexities and deviations as well as all the authentic achievements of humanity – to the shape of things which man and the world are, in the end, to come to accept. It will be accepted because of the indubitable fact that the affairs of man and the world reach consummation in the hands of God, Father, Son and Holy Spirit, who embraces and penetrates the entire world, for "in him we live and move and have our being" (Acts 17,28). The great German poet said, in *Faust*, that Satan is a force that always desires what is evil, whereas the good always goes into action.

2. *"So that God may be all in all"*

In considering this eschatological view of the consummation of all things in Christ, the second Vatican Council expresses itself as follows: "The shape of this world, deformed as it is by sin, will certainly pass away. We do know, from revelation, that God is preparing a new dwelling-place and a new earth in which justice will abide (cf 2 Cor 5,2; 2 Pet 3,13); its happiness will more than amply satisfy all the longings for peace that spring up in the hearts of men. Then, with death conquered, the sons of God will be brought to life again in Christ, and what was sown in weakness and corruption will be clothed in incorruptibility (cf 1 Cor 15,42.53); charity and its fruits will endure (cf 1 Cor 13,8; 3,14) and the whole of the reality created by God expressly for men (cf Rom 8,19–21) will be freed from the slavery of vanity" (*Gaudium et spes*, n.39).

And then: "After we have done as the Lord commanded, and in his Spirit have spread over the whole earth all that is good – human dignity, brotherhood and freedom, and all the good fruits of nature and of our activity – we shall find them all once again, but cleansed of all stain, illumined and transfigured, when Christ hands back to the Father 'the eternal and universal kingdom: a kingdom of truth and life, of holiness and grace, a kingdom of justice, love and peace' (Preface of the Feast of Christ the King). Here on earth that kingdom is already present in mystery; but with the coming of the Lord it will reach perfection" (n.39).

Here is another picture of the final consummation:

"Christ, having made himself obedient unto death and being therefore exalted by the Father (cf Phil 2,8–9), entered into the glory of his kingdom; to him all things are made subject, until he subjects himself and all creatures to the Father, so that God may be all in all (cf 1 Cor 15,27–28)" (*Lumen gentium*, n.36).

There we have the definition of the ultimate reality, the *eschaton*, the final consummation. It is effected not by the world or by man but by Christ. It is Christ who makes all things subject to the Father. And this "making subject" is inseparable from his own filial "submission" to the Father, as the Apostle teaches us (1 Cor 3,23): "You belong to Christ and Christ belongs to God". The trinitarian mystery, the unity of the godhead, the most perfect *communio personarum:* the unity of the Father and the Word in the uncreated Gift, remains divinely transcendent.

At the same time this trinitarian mystery becomes the ultimate dimension of the affairs of men and the world; and thanks to the Son having made all things subject to the Father in the Holy Spirit, the world once again plays its full part in the mystery of God, because God will be "all in all".

It is within the mystery of the final consummation that we have to seek the explanation of heaven; and there is little difficulty in finding it. But we also have to seek there the explanation of hell; it too belongs in the mystery of the final consummation of man and the world in Christ. Can man and his experience provide some clues? The whole inner reality of conscience is certainly relevant. We have already seen that conscience not only pronounces the verdict: "this action is a bad one" but also inflicts inner punishment. So it is quite correct to speak of conscience as a worm "gnawing at one's vitals". Indeed, Christ says of those condemned: "where the worm never dies and the fire is never quenched" (Mk 9,48); because remorse can burn too.

All the same, conscience alone does not tell the whole story about the mystery of hell; for we know from the Gospel that hell is not simply the state of having to endure the pangs

of a remorseful conscience but also the mystery of being in a
state of separation from God (cf, for example, Mt 25,41).
This mystery can be explained only on the basis of the truth
that man is called to communion, to a share in the fulness of
the trinitarian life of God, the *communio personarum*.
Separation is the opposite of communion. "When the Lord
Jesus prayed to the Father 'that all may be one'
(Jn 17,21–22), thus opening up for us horizons that are
beyond human reasoning, he implied a certain similarity
between the unity of the divine persons and the unity of the
sons of God in truth and charity" (*Gaudium et spes*, n.24).

The vocation to communion – in which persons offer one
another gifts of truth and love as in the case of the divine
Persons – is deeply ingrained in man. The Son of God came
into this world in order to reveal to mankind this sublime
vocation to unity in truth by way of charity. That is why
Jesus declared charity to be the greatest of all the commandments, making it central to his Gospel (Mk 12,28–31)
and predicting that it would determine his final judgment
(Mt 25,34–35). This judgment is in full accord with the
structure of the human conscience; indeed one might say that
thanks to conscience the whole structure of the person leans
in an eschatological direction. And this judgment is also in
full accord with the divine economy operating within the
affairs of man and the world, because "the Father judges
nobody but has entrusted all judgment to the Son" (Jn 5,22),
to the one who is to make all things subject to the Father,
subjecting himself as well, so that God may be "all in all".
When the Holy Spirit, the comforter, comes, he will convince
the world of the rightness of this judgment: "When he comes
– said Jesus in the upper room – he will convince the world
about sin, justice and judgment: about sin, because they do
not believe in me; about justice, because I am going to the
Father and you will no longer see me; and about judgment,
because the prince of this world is already condemned"
(Jn 16,8–11).

And so all who lay themselves open to the action of the

Holy Spirit are firmly convinced that the world is indeed progressing towards the day of the last judgment, which God the Father has entrusted to his Son.

3. *"He has entrusted all judgment to the Son"*

In his most impressive eschatological discourse, the Son drew for us a picture of that judgment. It is unforgettable, but we would do well to read it again in the context of this retreat of ours:

"When the Son of man comes in his majesty with all the angels, he will sit on the throne of his glory. And all the nations will be gathered together before him, but he will separate them one from another as the shepherd separates the sheep from the goats; and he will put the sheep on his right and the goats on his left. Then the king will say to those on his right: 'Come, you who are blessed by my Father, take possession of the kingdom prepared for you since the creation of the world. Because I was hungry and you gave me food; I was thirsty and you gave me drink; I was homeless and you gave me shelter; I was naked and you clothed me; sick and you visited me; in prison and you came to find me'. Then the just will reply: 'Lord, when did we see you hungry and give you food; thirsty and give you drink? When did we see you homeless and give you shelter, or naked and clothe you? When did we see you sick or in prison and come to visit you?'. And he will answer them: 'Truly I tell you, every time you did this for one of the least of these brethren of mine, you did it for me'. Finally he will say to those on his left: 'Go far from me, you who are accursed, to the everlasting fire prepared for the devil and his angels. For I was hungry and you gave me nothing to eat; I was thirsty and you gave me nothing to drink: I was homeless and you gave me no shelter; naked and you did not clothe me; sick and in prison and you did not visit me'. Then they too will reply: 'Lord, when did we ever see you hungry or thirsty or homeless or naked or sick or in prison and not help you?' But he will answer them: 'Truly I tell you: each time you failed to do this for one of the least of my brethren, you failed to do it for me'. And they will go to everlasting torment, while the just will go to everlasting life" (Mt 25,31–46).

"When the sun sets on my life I shall be judged on love", said St John of the Cross in all the eloquence of his mysticism. But Christ's eschatological discourse was addressed to every man and every age; it transcends all barriers as it outlines the form to be taken by the con- summation in which he, the Christ, is to make himself and all things subject to the Father so that "God may be all in all".

But will God really be all in all, given that the last judgment entrusted by the Father to the Son will award not only salvation, union with God, but also damnation?

"Go far from me, you who are accursed!" (Mt 25,41). Let us go back to the beginning of the covenant and recall that first awesome pronouncement: "I shall put enmity ..." (Gen 3,15) and the first curse (Gen 3,14). They were awesome because they were spoken by the heart of the Father. And now let us consider once again Christ's dis- course in which he depicts himself eventually separating those who are saved from those who are damned. Will God be all in all if in the final consummation – when the Son will make himself and all things subject to the Father in the Holy Spirit – there is to be this division, this contradiction?

It is well known that some people, Origen for one[2], have tried to go beyond this testimony left us by "Jesus Christ, the faithful witness, the first-born from among the dead, the ruler of the kings of the earth" (Rev 1,5).

Perhaps in the light of the truth that "God is love" (1 Jn 4,8.16) they were tentatively reaching out towards some later phase of the history of salvation – not disclosed in revelation and the scriptures – which might put an end to this separation between those who are saved and those who are damned.

All the same, besides being love God is also justice. He is

divine justice. The interplay of love and justice within the fulness of divine perfection, how they govern the choices made within the unity of Father, Son and Holy Spirit, remains an impenetrable mystery. But it is in the light of this mystery that we can understand what is meant by the Son handing back to the Father, in the final consummation, the whole truth of human knowledge and awareness and the whole truth of the history of salvation of the world.

God – who is the supreme mystery of justice in love and love in justice – *will* be all in all: whether in those who are on his right or in those who are on his left. The love that made all things in Christ, "amor Dei usque ad contemptum sui", did not deprive the creature of freedom, of the possibility of choosing, of the right to self-determination. Christ's eschatological discourse makes it clear that at the final consummation of the history of man and the world the "amor sui usque ad contemptum Dei" will still be present; and that type of love will reap its own harvest of definitive condemnation.

4. *"Gloria Dei vivens homo"*

The Son will hand all things back to the Father in the Holy Spirit. And this is what will make the consummation the "perfectum opus laudis". The glory of God is the prime norm of the whole of reality, and the consummation of all things will depend upon the degree to which God's glory has been made manifest. Glory is the irradiation of good, the reflecting of all perfection. And in one way it is also the inner atmosphere of the deity, the godhead. God lives in glory and transfuses this glory in all that he does. All his works are full of his glory: creation, redemption, sanctification, consummation. In a very special way God transmits this glory to man. The glory of God is living man; the glory of God is man alive. And God also leads man towards glory. Man's inner experience bound up with his conscience testifies to this, although the glory is limited to what human nature is capable of. The human conscience does not only accuse man and subject him to gnawing remorse; it also commends and praises him, and "love rejoices in the truth" (1 Cor 13,6). In man's estimation the silent but positive approval given him by his own quiet conscience far outweighs the most appalling suffering. We can think of men who even under torture have refused to betray their own conscience; we can think of the first Christians who refused to deny Christ because Christ had become their conscience. Even in human society at large there is this tendency to applaud any noble and worthy act; although the tendency here is less than steady, threatened as it is at every turn by subjectivism of all kinds and by a utilitarian outlook on life. But even history rejoices when it can manifest the true glory of man.

This glory is desired more by God than by man. He alone is capable of manifesting the glory of creation, of revealing the glory of man in the mirror of his truth and thus in the dimensions of the final consummation – which is the "perfectum opus laudis". All of that is possible, all of that will become a reality when we see him face to face as we are seen by him – in all the truth and with all the love "in communione personarum". "Our knowledge now is only partial, and our prophecy too is only partial. But when perfect knowledge of God comes to us, all that is only partial will disappear. Just as I, when I was a child, spoke like a child, whereas now that I have become a man I have laid aside childish ways. We now see things only as if in a dull mirror; but then we shall see face to face; now I know only imperfectly, but then I shall know perfectly, as I am known myself. So three things remain to us: faith, hope and charity; but the greatest of all is charity" (1 Cor 13,9–13).

Charity. Love. The fount and fulness of God's glory in man and man's glory in God. Charity "is patient and kind. Charity is not envious; it does not boast or grow conceited; it is not rude or self-indulgent; it does not take offence or bear any grudge; it takes no pleasure in injustice but rejoices in the truth. It excuses all things, believes all things, hopes all things and endures all things. Charity will never end" (1 Cor 13,4–8).

"God is love" (1 Jn 4,8.16). The glory of God is man alive.

Notes

1. St Irenaeus, *Adv. haer.* IV, 20,5–7.
2. Cf the texts concerning the *apokatastasis* in Origen in: J.A. Fischer, Studien zum Todesgedanken in der alten Kirche, Munich 1956.

XXI.

Via Crucis

In this meditation we shall try to follow in the Lord's footsteps along the way leading from Pilate's praetorium to the 'place of a skull', in Hebrew Golgotha (Jn 19,17). To this day pilgrims to the Holy Land from all over the world still follow that way. Your Holiness once followed it too, surrounded by an enormous crowd – people from Jerusalem as well as pilgrims from far afield. Historically our Lord Jesus Christ's *Via crucis* has always been associated with the places through which he passed himself. Yet through the centuries it has also been carried over to many other places where believers in the divine Master are set on following him in spirit on his way through Jerusalem. At some shrines, like the one at Kalwaria Zebrzydowska already mentioned, devotion to the Passion has inspired the faithful to reconstruct the *Via crucis* in a set of stations far distant one from the next. Usually the stations in our churches are fourteen in number, as in Jerusalem between the praetorium and the Holy Sepulchre. We are now going to pause awhile in spirit at each of those stations and meditate on the mystery of Christ burdened with the cross.

1st Station

Pilate's verdict was pronounced under pressure from the priests and the crowd. The sentence of death by crucifixion was meant to calm their fury and meet their clamorous demand of "Crucify him! Crucify him!" The Roman praetor thought he could dissociate himself from the sentence by washing his hands, just as he had evaded what had been said by Christ – who identified his kingdom with the truth, with witness to the truth (Jn 18,37). In both instances Pilate was trying to preserve his own independence, to remain somehow "not involved". So it may have seemed to him, on the surface. But the cross to which Jesus of Nazareth was condemned, like the truth he told about his kingdom, was to strike deep into the Roman praetor's soul. All this was a reality in the face of which one cannot remain uninvolved, on the side-lines.

When Jesus, the Son of God, was interrogated about his kingdom and, because of his kingdom, was judged guilty by men and condemned to death, his final testimony began: he was about to demonstrate that "God loved the world *so much* ...".

We have this testimony before us, and we know that we are not allowed to wash our hands of it.

2nd Station

The execution, the implementation of the sentence, is beginning. Christ condemned to death must be burdened with the cross just like two other men who are to undergo the same punishment: "he was numbered among the male-factors" (Is 53,12). Christ draws near to the cross, his body atrociously bruised and lacerated, blood trickling down his face from his head crowned with thorns. *Ecce homo!* In him there is all the truth foretold by the prophets about the Son of man, the truth predicted by Isaiah about the servant of Yahweh: "He was wounded for our iniquities ... in his wounds there is healing for us" (Is 53,5). And in him there is also an amazing sequel: here is what man has done to his God. Pilate says: "Ecce homo!" (Jn 19,5): "Look what you have done to this man!" But there seems to be another voice speaking as well, a voice that seems to be saying: "Look what you have done, in this man, to your God!"

It is very moving, this voice we can hear from centuries

away in the background of what comes to us through knowledge of the faith. *Ecce homo!*

Jesus "called the Messiah" (Mt 27,17) takes the cross on his shoulders (Jn 19,17). The execution has begun.

3rd Station

Jesus falls under the weight of the cross. He falls to the ground. He does not resort to his superhuman force, nor does he resort to the power of the angels. "Do you think that I cannot pray to my Father, who would at once send me more than twelve legions of angels?" (Mt 26,53). He does not ask for that. Having accepted the cup from his Father's hands (Mk 14,36) he is resolved to drink it to the end. He wills it no other way. And so he has no thoughts of any superhuman force, although such forces are at his disposal. People who have seen him when he exercised power over human infirmities, crippling diseases and even death may well, in their grief, be wondering "What now? Is he repudiating all that?" "We had hoped", the Emmaus disciples were to say a few days later (cf Lk 24,21). "If you are the Son of God ..." the members of the Sanhedrin were to fling at him. "He saved others but he cannot save himself" (Mk 15,31; Mt 27,42) the crowd was to yell.

And he accepts these provocations, which seem to undermine the whole meaning of his mission, his teaching, his miracles. He accepts them all, for he is determined not to combat them. To be insulted is what he wills. To stagger and fall under the weight of the cross is what he wills. He wills it all. To the end, down to the very last detail, he is true to his undertaking: "Not my will but yours be done" (cf Mk 14,36).

God will draw the salvation of humanity from Christ's falls under the weight of the cross.

4th Station

The Mother. Mary meets her son along the way of the cross. His cross becomes her cross, his humiliation is her humiliation, the public scorn is on her shoulders. This is the way of the world. This is how it must seem to the people around, and this is how her heart reacts: "A sword will pierce your soul" (Lk 2,35). The words spoken when Jesus was 40 days old are now coming true. They are reaching complete fulfilment. And so, pierced by that invisible sword, Mary moves towards her son's Calvary, her own Calvary. Christian devotion sees her with this sword through her heart, and depicts and sculpts her thus. Mother of sorrows!

"You who shared his suffering!" say the faithful, with an inner awareness that the mystery of this suffering can be expressed in no other way. Although the pain is proper to her, striking deep into her maternal heart, the full truth of this suffering can be expressed only in terms of shared suffering – 'com-passion'. That word is part of the mystery; it expresses unity with the suffering of the Son.

5th Station

Simon of Cyrene, called upon to carry the cross (cf Mk 15,21; Lk 23,26), doubtless had no wish to do so. He was forced to. He made his way alongside Christ, bearing the weight himself. When the condemned man's shoulders became too weak, he lent him his. He moved along very close to Jesus, closer than Mary, closer than John who – though he too was a man – was not called upon to help. They called on him, Simon of Cyrene, father of Alexander and Rufus (Mk 15,21). They summoned him, they compelled him.

How long did he go on resenting being forced into this? How long did he go on walking beside this condemned man yet making it clear that he had nothing in common with him, nothing to do with his crime, nothing to do with his punishment? How long did he go on like that, divided within himself, a barrier of indifference getting between him and the man who was suffering? "I was naked, I was thirsty, I was in prison" (cf Mt 25,35–36), I have carried the cross ... and: Did you carry it with me? ... Did you really carry it with me right to the end?

We do not know. St Mark simply records the names of the Cyrenian's sons, and tradition has it that they were members of the christian community close to St Peter (cf Rom 16,13).

6th Station

Tradition has bequeathed us Veronica. Perhaps she is a counterpart to the story of the man from Cyrene. For although, being a woman, she could not physically carry the cross or be called upon to do so, there is no doubt that she did in fact carry the cross with Jesus: she carried it in the only way open to her at the time, in obedience to the dictates of her heart: she wiped his face.

Tradition has it that an imprint of Christ's features remained on the handkerchief she used. This detail seems fairly easily explainable: because the handkerchief was impregnated with blood and sweat, traces and outlines could remain.

Yet a different significance can be attributed to this detail if it is considered in the light of Christ's eschatological discourse. There will undoubtedly be many who will ask: "Lord, when did we ever do these things for you?" And Jesus will reply: "Whatever you did for the least of these brethren of mine, you did for me" (cf Mt 25,37–40). In fact the Saviour leaves his imprint on every single act of charity, as on Veronica's handkerchief.

7th Station

"I am a worm, not a man, scorned by all, the laughing-stock of the mob" (Ps 22(21),6): the words of the Psalmist-prophet come wholly true in these steep, narrow little streets of

Jerusalem in the last hours before the Passover. And we know that those hours before the feast are unnerving, with the streets teeming with people. This is the context in which the words of the Psalmist are coming true, even though nobody gives this a thought. Certainly it passes unnoticed by those who are displaying their scorn, people for whom this Jesus of Nazareth – who is now falling for the second time – has become a laughing-stock.

And he wills all this, he wills fulfilment of the prophecy. So he falls, exhausted by all the effort. He falls in accordance with the will of the Father, a will expressed in the words of the prophet. He falls in accordance with his own will, so that "the scriptures may be fulfilled" (Mt 26,54): "I am a worm, not a man" (Ps 22(21),6). So, not even "Ecce homo" but something much less, much worse.

A worm creeps and crawls along the ground whereas man, the king among creatures, strides high above it. A worm will gnaw even at wood: like a worm, remorse for sin gnaws at the human conscience. Remorse for the second fall.

8th Station

Here is the call to repentance, true repentance, sorrow, in the truth of the evil that has been committed. Jesus says to the daughters of Jerusalem who are weeping at the sight of him: "Do not weep for me, but weep for yourselves and for your children" (Lk 23,28). One cannot merely scrape away at the surface of evil; one has to get down to its roots, its causes, the inner truth of the conscience.

This is the meaning of the Jesus who carries the cross, who always "knew what is in man" (cf Jn 2,25) and always does know. This is why he must always be for us the nearest onlooker of all, the one who sees all our actions and is aware of all the verdicts passed on them by our consciences. Perhaps he even makes us understand that these verdicts have to be carefully thought out, reasonable, objective (for he says "Do not weep") but at the same time bound up with all that this truth contains; he warns us of this because he is the one who carries the cross.

Lord, let me know how to live and walk in the truth!

9th Station

"He became humbler still, making himself obedient even to death, death on the cross" (Phil 2,8). Every station along this way is a milestone of that obedience and self-deprivation. We appreciate the scale of that self-deprivation when we begin to study the words of the prophet: "The Lord has laid on him the iniquity of us all. ... Like sheep we were all going astray, each following his own track; but the Lord has laid on him the iniquity of us all" (Is 53,6).

We can appreciate the extent of that self-deprivation when we see Jesus falling for the third time under the cross. We can appreciate it when we think carefully who it is falling, who it is lying in the dusty road under the cross, at the feet of a hostile crowd that spares him no insult or humiliation.... .

Who is it who has fallen? Who is Jesus Christ? "His nature was divine, yet he did not cling to his equality with God but preferred to deprive himself of it, taking the nature of a slave and becoming as men are; and after taking on human nature he became humbler still, making himself obedient even to death, death on a cross" (Phil 2,6–8).

10th Station

When Jesus is stripped of his clothes at Golgotha (cf Mk 15,24) our thoughts turn once again to his mother: they go back in time to the first days of this body which now, even before the crucifixion, is one mass of wounds (Is 52,14). The mystery of the Incarnation: the Son of God derives his body from the Virgin's womb (cf Mt 1,23; Lk 1,26–28). The Son of God speaks to the Father in the words of the Psalmist: "You wanted neither sacrifices nor burnt offerings ... but you have shaped a body for me" (Ps 40(39),6; Heb 10,6.5).

The man's body expresses his soul. Christ's body expresses his love for the Father: "Then I said: See, I come ... to do your will, O God" (Ps 40(39),7; Heb 10,7). "I always do what is pleasing to him" (Jn 8,29). With every wound, every spasm of pain, every wrenched muscle, every trickle of blood, with all the exhaustion in its arms, all the bruises and lacerations on its back and shoulders, this unclothed body is carrying out the will of both Father and Son. It carries out the Father's will when it is stripped naked and subjected to torture, when it takes unto itself the immeasurable pain of humanity defiled and profaned.

Men's bodies are defiled and profaned in a number of ways.

At this station we must think of the Mother of Christ, because in her womb, before her eyes and at her hands the body of the Son of God was adored to the full.

11th Station

"They have pierced my hands and my feet, I can count all my bones" (Ps 22(21),16–17). "I can count ...": how prophetic those words turned out to be! And yet we know that this body is a ransom. The whole of this body, hands, feet and every bone, is a priceless ransom. The whole of this man is in a state of utmost tension: bones, muscles, nerves, every organ, every cell is stretched and strained to breaking-point. "I, when I am lifted up from the earth, will draw all men to myself" (Jn 12,32). Therein lies the full reality of the crucifixion. And part of this reality is the terrible tension driving its way into hands, feet and every bone: driving its way into his entire body which, nailed like a mere thing to the beams of the cross, is about to be utterly 'voided' in the convulsive agony of death. And the whole of the world which Jesus wills to draw to himself comes into the reality of the cross. The world is dependent on the gravitation of this body, which inertia is causing to sink lower and lower.

The Passion of Christ crucified resides in this gravitation.

"You are from below, I am from above" (Jn 8,23). From the cross he says: "Father, forgive them, because they do not know what they are doing" (Lk 23,34).

12th Station

Nailed to the cross, pinned immobile in that terrible position, Jesus invokes the Father (cf Mk 15,34; Lk 23,46). All his invocations bear witness that he is one with the Father. "The Father and I are one" (Jn 10,30); "Anyone who has seen me has seen the Father" (Jn 14,9); "My Father has never ceased to work to this day, and I work too" (Jn 5,17).

Here we have the finest, the most sublime work of the Son in union with the Father. Yes: in union, in the most perfect union possible, precisely at the moment when he cries: "Eloi, Eloi, lama sabachthani" – "My God, my God, why have you forsaken me?" (Mk 15,34; Lk 23,46). This work finds expression in the verticality of the body stretched against the perpendicular beam of the cross and in the horizontality of the arms stretched along the transverse timber. To see those arms one would think that in the effort they expend they embrace all humanity and all the world.

They do indeed embrace.

Here is the man. Here is God himself. "In him we live and move and have our being" (Acts 17,28). In him: in those arms outstretched along the transverse beam of the cross.

The mystery of redemption.

13th Station

When the body is taken down from the cross and laid in the Mother's arms, in our mind's eye we glimpse again the moment when Mary accepted the message brought by the angel Gabriel: "You will conceive in your womb and give birth to a son whom you will call Jesus ... the Lord God will give him the throne of David, his father ... and his reign will never end" (Lk 1,31–33). All that Mary said was: "Let it all happen to me as you have said" (Lk 1,38), as though even then she had wanted to express what she is undergoing now.

In the mystery of redemption, grace – the gift of God himself – is interwoven with the "payment" made by the human heart. In this mystery we are enriched by a gift from on high (Jas 1,17) and at the same time "paid for" by the ransom of the Son of God (cf 1 Cor 6,20; 7,23; Acts 20,28). And Mary, who more than anyone else was enriched with gifts from on high, pays even more dearly. With her heart.

Inseparable from this mystery is the extraordinary promise formulated by Simeon during the presentation of Jesus in the temple: "A sword will pierce your heart, so that the thoughts of many hearts may be laid bare" (Lk 2,35).

This too comes true. How many human hearts bleed for the heart of this Mother who has paid so dearly!

Once again Jesus is in her arms, as he was in the stable in Bethlehem (cf Lk 2,16), during the flight into Egypt (cf Mt 2,14), at Nazareth (cf Lk 2,39–40). Pietà.

14th Station

From the moment when man, because of sin, was banished from the tree of life (cf Gen 3), the earth became a burial ground. For every human being there is a tomb. A vast planet of tombs.

Close to Calvary there was a tomb belonging to Joseph of Arimathea (cf Mt 27,60). In it, with Joseph's consent, the body of Jesus was placed after being taken down from the cross (cf Mk 15,42–46). They laid it there in haste in order that the burial might be completed before the feast of Passover which began at sunset (cf Jn 19,31).

In one of the innumerable tombs scattered all over the continents of this planet of ours the Son of God, the man Jesus Christ, conquered death with death. "O mors! ero mors tua!" (1st Antiphon, Lauds, Holy Saturday). The tree of life from which man was banished because of sin is newly revealed to men in the body of Christ. "If anyone eats this bread he will have eternal life; and the bread that I shall give for the life of the world is my flesh" (Jn 6,51).

In spite of the fact that our planet is constantly being studded with fresh tombs, becoming more and more a burial ground in which man who emerged from dust returns to dust (cf Gen 3,19), nonetheless all who look to the tomb of Jesus Christ live in Resurrection hope.

XXII.

Conclusion

1. A sign of contradiction

Now that we have reached the last meditation, let us try to pick up the thread that first attracted our attention, the guiding thread we have had in mind from the start.

Forty days after his birth Jesus, son of Mary, was presented at the temple in Jerusalem in accordance with Old Testament law (cf Lk 2,22–38). When Mary and Joseph entered the temple to go through the presentation rite, the old man Simeon took the child in his arms and spoke the prophetic words (cf Lk 2,29–32) which the Church recites every evening during Compline: "A light to shine for the gentiles", and then, turning to Mary, referred to him in the words we chose as the leit-motif of our retreat: "He is set for the fall and the rising of many in Israel, and as a sign of contradiction ..." (Lk 2,34).

Nearly two thousand years have passed but the words then spoken have lost none of their validity or relevance. It is becoming more and more evident that those words sum up most felicitously the whole truth about Jesus Christ, his mission and his Church. "A sign of contradiction". In earlier meditations we tried to sketch some of the forms this contradiction can take while we were trying to understand what it stems from. All of that guided us through the meditations on the great works of God and on the "mystery of man" contained in them.

It is in Jesus Christ that both the "magnalia Dei" (Acts 2,11; cf, for example, Sir 18,5; 2 Mac 3,34) and the most profound dimension of man's mystery are most easily accessible to men's intellects and hearts. That is why in this last meditation we want to look once again in loving faith at what occurred in the temple forty days after his birth.

The times in which we are living provide particularly strong confirmation of the truth of what Simeon said: Jesus is both the light that shines for mankind and at the same time a sign of contradiction. If now – on the threshold of the last quarter-century before the second millennium, after the second Vatican Council, and in the face of the terrible experiences the human family has undergone and is still undergoing – Jesus Christ is once again revealing himself to men as the light of the world, has he not also become at one and the same time that sign which, more than ever, men are resolved to oppose?

Let us think again about all that the world and present-day man are living through, all that undoubtedly causes particular distress of soul to the successor of Peter, to whom the Lord entrusted the keys of the kingdom of heaven saying: "Whatever you bind on earth shall be bound in heaven too; and whatever you loose on earth shall be loosed in heaven too" (Mt 16,19); "You are Peter (that is, the rock)" (Mt 16,18). This earth of ours seems smaller now, distances have shrunk (cf *Gaudium et spes*, n. 5), even the moon – one of earth's satellites – has been trodden by the feet of men. And because of this mutual growing-closer which we owe to the means of transport and the mass media we are better able to discern the paths followed by that opposition to Christ Jesus, his Gospel and the Church. It is difficult to collect up and put before you all the ways in which Simeon's prophecy has come true in one form or another, but we shall try to make some of them evident.

In men of today there undoubtedly is one form of contradiction which one may illustrate with the parable of Dives and Lazarus (cf Lk 16,19–31). Jesus is on the side of Lazarus. His kingdom will come in this world in accordance with the programme of the beatitudes (cf Mt 5,3–10), and we know that the poor are the blessed ones (Lk 6,20), the poor in spirit (Mt 5,3), the meek, those who hunger and thirst for justice and those who weep. Those who take pity, too, are blessed. The great poverty of many peoples, first and foremost the poverty of the peoples of the Third World, hunger, economic exploitation, colonialism – which is not confined to the Third World – all this is a form of opposition to Christ on the part of the powerful, irrespective of political regimes and cultural traditions. This form of contradiction of Christ often goes hand-in-hand with a partial acceptance of religion, of Christianity and the Church, an acceptance of Christ as an element present in culture, morality and even education. Dives appealed to Abraham and turned to him as Father (Lk 16,24).

Certainly there is in this world a powerful reserve of faith, and also a considerable margin of freedom for the Church's mission. But often it is no more than a margin. One need only take note of the principal tendencies governing the means of social communication, one need only pay heed to what is passed over in silence and what is shouted aloud, one need only lend an ear to what encounters most opposition, to perceive that even where Christ is accepted there is at the same time opposition to the full truth of his Person, his mission and his Gospel. There is a desire to "re-shape" him, to adapt him to suit mankind in this era of progress and make him fit in with the programme of modern civilisation – which is a programme of consumerism and not of transcendental ends. There is opposition to him from those standpoints, and the truth proclaimed and recorded in his name is not tolerated (cf Acts 4,10.12.18). This opposition to Christ which goes hand-in-hand with paying him lip-service – and it is to be found also among those who call themselves his disciples – is particularly symptomatic of our own times.

Yet that is not the only form of contradiction of Christ. Alongside what can be called "indirect contradiction" – and incidentally there are many variations on it, many shades and blends – alongside that there is another form of contradiction probably arising out of the same historical

basis as the first one – and therefore more or less a result of
that first one. It is a form of direct opposition to Christ, an
undisguised rejection of the Gospel, a flat denial of the truth
about God, man and the world as proclaimed by the Gospel.
This denial sometimes takes on a brutal character. We know
that there are still some countries where churches of all
denominations are closed, where priests are sentenced to
death for having administered baptism. Perhaps in those
areas of persecution there are still traces of the ancient
christian catacombs, of the circuses where witnesses to Christ
were thrown to the lions. But present-day persecution, the
kind typical of these last years of the 20th century, occurs in
a context quite different from that of ancient times, and it
therefore has a quite different significance.

We are living in an age in which the whole world
proclaims freedom of conscience and religious freedom, and
also in an age in which the battle against religion – defined
as "the opium of the people" – is being fought in such a way
as to avoid, as far as possible, making any new martyrs. And
so the programme for today is one of face-saving persecution:
persecution is declared non-existent and full religious
freedom is declared assured. What is more, this programme
has succeeded in giving many people the impression that it is
on the side of Lazarus against the rich man, that it is
therefore on the same side as Christ, whereas in fact it is
above all against Christ. Can we really say: "above all"? We
would so much like to be able to affirm the opposite. But
unfortunately the facts demonstrate clearly that the battle
against religion *is* being fought, and that this battle still
constitutes an untouchable point of dogma in the programme. It also seems as if, for the attainment of this
"heaven upon earth", it is most of all necessary to deprive
man of the strength he draws on in Christ (cf Rom 1,16;
1 Cor 1,18; 2 Cor 13,4; Phil 4,16): this "strength" has indeed
been condemned as weakness, unworthy of man. Unworthy ... troublesome, rather. The man who is strong with the
strength given him by the faith does not easily allow himself

to be thrust into the anonymity of the collective (cf 2 Cor 12,9).

2. *The mystery of Mary*

And so in the vast panorama of the times in which we live, in the age to which we belong, Simeon's prophecy of Jesus Christ as a "sign of contradiction" seems to ring resoundingly true. We know that immediately after speaking those words Simeon turned to Mary, in a way linking the prophecy about the Son with the one about the Mother: "And a sword will pierce your soul, so that the thoughts of many hearts may be laid bare". With the old man's words in mind we too turn our gaze from the Son to the Mother, from Jesus to Mary. The mystery of this bond which unites her with Christ, the Christ who is "a sign of contradiction", is truly amazing.

In revelation, in holy scripture, Mary has as it were two dimensions. The first is that of a humble, lowly daughter of Israel (cf Zeph 3,12) for whom the Lord did great things (cf Lk 1,49). This is the Mary we know from Luke's and John's gospels: Mary at Nazareth (Lk 1,26–50), Mary at Bethlehem (Mt 2,1–12; Lk 2,4–20), Mary fleeing to Egypt (Mt 2,13–14.19–21) and then again at Nazareth (Mt 2,23; Lk 2,39–52). It is the Mary who asks her 12-year-old son: "Why did you do this?" (Lk 2,48). It is the Mary at Cana in Galilee who gets worried: "They have no more wine" (Jn 2,3), and then turns to the servants and says: "Do whatever he tells you". Finally it is the Mary about whom somebody says to Jesus: "Your mother and your brethren are outside wanting to speak to you" (Mt 12,47) and "Blessed is the womb that bore you and the breasts you sucked" (Lk 11,27). And notwithstanding all that he answers: "Who is my mother, and who are my brethren? ... Anyone who does the will of my Father is my brother and my sister and my mother" (Mt 12,48–50).

This is she, Mary, daughter of Israel, "united, in descent

from Adam, with all men needing salvation" (*Lumen gentium*, n. 53). That is the teaching of Vatican II, which later tells us: "She moved forward in her pilgrimage of faith and loyally maintained her union with her Son all the way to the cross where, in keeping with a divine plan, she stood (cf Jn 19,25), suffering grievously with her only Son and in her mother's heart associating herself with his sacrifice, lovingly consenting to the immolation of the victim to whom she had given birth; and finally the same Christ Jesus gave her as mother to the disciple, saying: "Woman, here is your son" (cf Jn 19,26–27)" (*Lumen gentium*, n. 58).

This is she, Mary. We know her life by heart; indeed the details to be remembered are few. A life that was almost always hidden. We know how little of what was said by the Mother of God is recorded in the Gospel. So let us, with the Church, contemplate her mystery: "Mary, a daughter of Adam, in consenting to the divine message became the mother of Jesus; and in embracing God's salvific will, with her whole soul and without any burden of sin, she totally consecrated herself as handmaid of the Lord to the person and the work of her Son, serving the mystery of redemption in subservience to him and together with him by the grace of Almighty God. Hence many of the Fathers of early times declare in their preaching that 'the knot of Eve's disobedience was untied by Mary's obedience' " (*Lumen gentium*, n. 56).

These words sum up the whole of tradition, the testimony of the Fathers and the living faith of the Church. Guided by chapter VIII of the Constitution on the Church let us enter the second dimension of the truth about Mary. This humble servant of the Lord, the virgin-mother of Nazareth, hidden in the mystery of her Son, seems to move in God's plan beyond the humble bounds of her historical existence. The truth about her reaches right back to the origins of mankind, because it was then that certain words were spoken – words concerning the woman, mother of the Son who will crush the serpent's head (Gen 3,15); and the teaching of Vatican II refers to those words (*Lumen gentium*, n. 55). Mary is part of salvation history from the beginning, and she will remain part of it until the end. Indeed, the picture of the woman in the third chapter of Genesis is to be found again in the book of Revelation, in the context of the eschatological travail that will fall to the Church's lot until the end of time.

"Then a great sign appeared in heaven: a woman clothed with the sun, with the moon beneath her feet and on her head a crown of twelve stars; and being pregnant and in labour she cried aloud in the pains of childbirth. Meanwhile another sign appeared in heaven: a great dragon of the colour of fire, with seven heads and twelve horns; and seven diadems on its heads. Its tail dragged a third of the stars from the sky and swept them down to earth. Then the dragon stopped in front of the woman who was about to give birth, so as to devour the child as soon as it was born. And she gave birth to a male child, destined to guide and pasture all nations with a staff of iron, and her son was taken straight up to God and his throne" (Rev 12,1–5). This is fully in line with the book of Genesis: "I will place enmity between you and the woman, between your seed and her seed...". And here is what we read in Revelation: "Then war broke out in heaven. Michael and his angels fought the dragon. The dragon and his angels fought back, but they could not win and there was no longer any place for them in heaven. And the great dragon was hurled down, that old serpent called the devil and Satan, the deceiver of the whole world was hurled down, and his angels were hurled down with him" (Rev 12,7–10).

Then come words ("When the dragon found himself hurled down to the earth, he pursued the woman who had given birth to the male child") which are interpreted by P. Jankowski, a well-known expert on the book of Revelation and commentator of the Tyniec bible, as referring to attacks by Satan on the Church: "The attack on the Messiah having been repulsed, Satan proceeds to turn his attack against the Church".

"But the earth came to the help of the woman": a highly metaphorical sentence which is followed by other words suggesting a subsequent battle in the sense foreseen in the book of Genesis: "The earth opened its mouth and swallowed the river which the dragon had poured from its mouth. Then the dragon was enraged against the woman, and went to make war on the rest of her offspring, against those who obey God's commandments and remain faithful to the Gospel of Jesus" (Rev 12,15–17).

3. *"Signum magnum"*

"The earth came to the help of the woman" is metaphorical. Perhaps these words are meant to convey that man, the human race, will instinctively resort to self-defence when evil shows itself more openly, when its destructive dimension becomes more evident. A few years after the Council the Holy Father recalled the words from Revelation which occur so often in the liturgy, especially on the feast of the Assumption: "Signum magnum apparuit in coelo". Although the images in Revelation are metaphorical in character, these literary forms nonetheless express very simply and clearly what is a truth: the truth that there is a very close bond linking Mary, mother of the Messiah, and the Church[1]. The "woman" in Revelation represents both Mary and the Church – as is agreed by biblical scholars, theologians and above all christian tradition and the Church's magisterium. That is why Vatican II, in line with this wonderful tradition, gave prominence to the truth that "the Mother of God is a figure of the Church, a type ... in the order of faith, charity and perfect union with Christ. Indeed in the mystery of the Church, herself rightly called mother and virgin, the Blessed Virgin Mary led the way, giving herself as virgin and mother in a manner both eminent and special to herself" (*Lumen gentium*, n.63).

The Holy Father has proclaimed Mary Mother of the

Church,[2] and using this title has invoked her whom the Church venerates as the most sublime model she has.

Both holy scripture, so rich in metaphor as we have just found, and the experience of the faithful see the Mother of God as the one who in a very special way is united with the Church at the most difficult moments in her history, when the attacks on her become most threatening. And this is in full accord with the vision of the woman revealed in Genesis and Revelation. Precisely in periods when Christ, and therefore his Church, Pope, bishops, priests, religious and all the faithful become the sign which provokes the most implacable and premeditated contradiction, Mary appears particularly close to the Church, because the Church is always in a way her Christ, first the Christ-child and then the crucified and risen Christ.

If in such periods, such times in history, there arises a particular need to entrust oneself to Mary – as the Holy Father did on 8th December 1975, the 10th anniversary of the end of the Council – that need flows directly from the integral logic of the faith, from rediscovery of the whole divine economy and from understanding of its mysteries.

The Father in heaven demonstrated the greatest trust in mankind by giving mankind his Son (cf Jn 3,16). The human creature to whom he first entrusted him was Mary, the woman of the *proto-evangelium* (cf Gen 3,15), then Mary of Nazareth and Bethlehem. And until the end of time she will remain the one to whom God entrusts the whole of his mystery of salvation.

The woman of Revelation, "a great sign appeared in the heavens" (Rev 12,1). Within the dimensions of the universe the Son of God, the eternal Word, the Lord of the ages to come is her son and she is his mother. Therefore all that goes to make up what he bequeathed – the work of salvation, the Mystical Body of Christ, the People of God, the Church -- is taken care of, and always will be taken care of, by her – with the same fidelity and strength that she showed in taking care of her son: from the stable in Bethlehem, to Calvary and to the upper room on the day of Pentecost when the Church was born. Mary is present in all the vicissitudes of this Church. She is very close indeed to the wonderful mystery expressed by the *proto-evangelium*. She: a weak woman. "God chose the weak of this world to confound the powerful" (1 Cor 1,27).

Our times are marked by a great expectation. All who believe in Christ and worship the true God are seeking ways of coming closer to one another. They are seeking paths leading to unity, and their cry is: "Christ sets us free and unites us". The Church, the People of God, senses ever more profoundly that she is being called to this unity. The Church, the People of God, is at the same time the Mystical Body of Christ. St Paul likened the Church to the human body in order to describe more clearly its life and its unity. The human body is given its life and its unity by the mother. Mary, by the working of the Holy Spirit, gave unity to the human body of Christ. And that is why our hope today turns in a special way towards her, in these times of ours when the Mystical Body of Christ is being more fully reconstituted in unity.

By the end of the 1975 Holy Year we had already entered the last quarter-century of the two thousand years since the birth of Christ, a new Advent for the Church and for humanity. A time of expectation and also of one crucial temptation – in a way still the same temptation that we know of from the third chapter of Genesis, though in one sense more deep-rooted than ever. A time of great trial but also of great hope. For just such a time as this we have been given the sign: Christ, "sign of contradiction" (Lk 2,34). And the woman clothed with the sun: "A great sign in the heavens" (Rev 12,1).

Notes

1. Paul VI, Apostolic Exhortation, *Marialis Cultus*.
2. Cf *Credo Populi Dei*.